Following the River

Following the River

Traces of Red River Women

Lorri Neilsen Glenn

WOLSAK
& WYNN

Cover and interior design: Marijke Friesen
Author photograph: University of King's College
Typeset in: Minion
Printed by Ball Media, Brantford, Canada

The publisher gratefully acknowledges the support of the Canada
Council for the Arts, the Ontario Arts Council and the Government of Canada.

Wolsak and Wynn Publishers, Ltd.
280 James Street North
Hamilton, ON
Canada L8R 2L3

Library and Archives Canada Cataloguing in Publication
Glenn, Lorri Neilsen, author
     Following the river : traces of Red River women / Lorri
Neilsen Glenn.

Includes bibliographical references.
ISBN 978-1-928088-47-9 (softcover)

     1. Métis women—Manitoba—History. 2. Métis—Manitoba—
Ethnic identity. 3. Glenn, Lorri Neilsen. 4. Glenn, Lorri
Neilsen—Family. I. Title.

FC126.W6G54 2017   305.48'8970712743   C2017-904882-1

For Aunt Kay,
and for the women of Red River and Rupert's Land –
my grandmothers and their contemporaries –
mothers, daughters, sisters, cousins who travelled
between worlds: *âtayôhkanak*.
Thank you for your lives and
your teachings, my passages
into understanding.

This is your story
even though you haven't told it
all or don't know how to tell
parts of it yet. By starting the story
the story tells you, tells you how
to go on and how to look back.
– Marilyn Dumont, "the dimness of mothers and daughters"

Of telling the truth to the best of our abilities, of knowing how we got
here, of listening particularly to those who have been silenced in the past,
of seeing how the myriad fit together and break apart.
– Rebecca Solnit, *The Mother of All Questions*

CONTENTS

"Selkirk, Manitoba, 1908." SS *Premier*. Archives of Manitoba,
Loudon G. Wilson fonds, PR-1978-14, photo 429.

Selkirk, Manitoba, August 1908

Time slows down, then it flies.

Summer here is muggy, close and sticky. I imagine you on the gang-plank, turning around to wave at one or more of your children, now grown. Was it Nettie? Malvena? Other passengers, shaking their handkerchiefs in the smoky air, cheer as the SS *Premier* moves slowly away from the Selkirk dock to begin its cruise north. The wind picks up, cools the back of your neck, riffles hats and hair of the passengers, and drives mosquitoes away from everyone's damp skin.

Catherine Kennedy Couture, great-grandmother, in my mind's eye, over a century away.

It is 1908. Your husband, Antoine, is working as a cook almost one thousand kilometres north of here. You have paid the equivalent of a man's monthly wages for passage on this steamer, one of several that weave in and around inlets and islands on Lake Winnipeg, to dock days away at Warren's Landing, several kilometres from the mainland community of Norway House. It remains a mystery to me how, having raised eleven children largely on your own, you are able to afford the fare. It's a luxury cruise; wealthy tourists from Eastern Canada and the fast-growing city of Winnipeg are now able to see the land your ancestors have known for centuries.

Settlements have grown, everything is changing. The SS *Premier* passes Cooks Creek and the old St. Peter's Reserve northeast of Selkirk, where fishers set out stakes on lines they attach to stone-filled cans to alert them to the presence of a catch. Their grey huts and tents would be a marvel to those standing at the ship's guardrail, few of whom would know you had relatives there.

You'll stop at communities along the banks of Lake Winnipeg to "wood up" the steamer.

As the ship keeps its pace of five miles per hour, some passengers will go below, escaping sparks and ashes spewing from the stack. Some will have arrived from the East by railway, the iron horse bringing curiosity seekers and hopeful settlers along the southern section of what was once called Rupert's Land.

The breeze picks up, the steamer makes its way out of the mouth of the Red River and into lake waters. Like any of us on a voyage, you must be hoping for good weather. This is storm season.

Two years ago, almost to the day, the SS *Princess* sank off Swampy Island, taking six people with it. The storm rose, shattering the vessel as the captain tried in vain to turn it around. It was Canada's worst inland maritime disaster.

Your cabin is below with the cargo, and later you'll descend the crowded stairs to settle in. The ship is stocked with supplies for Norway House and farther north, as well as empty crates to be filled with rich fish harvests at Warren's Landing and brought south. On return trips, steamers – and before them, York boats – have been filled with finery, musical instruments, china, stoves, tools and household goods shipped from Europe.

I know so little about you.

Europe. In six years the Great War will break out. Your youngest, Edgar, will die from his wounds. You'll never see the winter of 1919, when influenza cut such a swath men drove carts along Manitoba streets to gather dead bodies to store in huts for burial in the spring.

In three years, your daughter Eleanore will marry Charles, an Irish-American who migrated north. You'll miss the wall of sweet peas in Eleanore's Saskatchewan garden, her Mason jars of jellied chicken and Saskatoon jam. You'll miss knowing your grandchildren, one of whom is my father.

In two days, the SS *Premier* will dock at Warren's Landing. Some passengers will take smaller vessels to Norway House, about fifty kilometres away. Others, like you, will stay at the landing. You'll spend time with Antoine in the boarding house, and when it's time to return to Selkirk, at least two of your adult children working there with Antoine will see you to the dock. For the trip home, everyone is required to board at night, ready for an early morning sail.

What happens next will be documented in newspapers across the globe – an event I learned about years ago from your granddaughter Kay, my centenarian aunt. It's a story that will tug at me, draw me to the river to uncover your past and the lives of your ancestors and other Red River women. As stories go, when I search for yours, I am searching for mine as well.

You are forty-nine years old this summer day. You were born either on St. Peter's Reserve, or in St. Andrews. Your father was a member of the Peguis Nation, signatories to Treaty 1, a Kennedy who travelled to Red River in the early 1800s. On your mother's side, you descend from maskêkowininiwak/ininiwak (Swampy Cree) near Hudson Bay. You're listed in the census, but I can find no official record of your birth.

For all the advances in science since you were born, we still cannot wrinkle time. And so, I'll begin by making my way to Selkirk to search for your story, hoping print records and artifacts survived.

As your granddaughter Kay reminds me, however, "There weren't the same rules then. People made things up."

This much I know: as you head out of the mouth of the Red River to open water on that warm August day, you won't come home alive.

Introduction

Woman on the River

Testamentum from the diary of William H. Keating, explorer:

But an object, which once riveted our attention, was the sight of a crazed woman standing alone in a canoe, which was steering with apparent ease. She had a tall commanding figure; a soft expression of melancholy beauty, such as often seen in the women of mixed European and Indian blood. Her dark eyes had, from the distorted state of her mind, received a wild and peculiarly interesting expression. She struck the water at irregular intervals with a long paddle which she held by the middle, singing at the same time a melancholy air, that struck our ear melodiously and sweetly, as we heard it from a distance. Perhaps, however, it was but the effect of an association of ideas, which lent a melancholy interest to her voice. She was the wife of one of the settlers. She was a half-breed, whose insanity was supposed to have sprung from a religious melancholy. Being one of those whom the missionaries had converted, she had become very pious, but her intellect was too frail for the doctrines which had been taught to her; in endeavoring to become familiar with them, she had been gradually affected with a malady, which at that time seemed incurable. While we were listening to this story, the wind heightened, the evening approached; all the canoes had disappeared from the river except hers, which she still kept on the stream, notwithstanding.

A Cord, However Slender

Who can speak or write about another? Who should? Especially when you're part of a culture responsible for the decimation, abuse, suppression and – let's face it – genocide of another cultural group?

In the early 1960s, John Howard Griffin published *Black Like Me,* a walk-the-walk sociological project to record the effects of passing as a black man. In 2015, Spokane's then–NAACP leader Rachel Dolezal faced challenges to her chosen Black identity when she was found to be the daughter of two Caucasian parents. Most Canadians have heard of Grey Owl, who passed as Indigenous over a century ago. In Quebec, a newly formed group called the Mikinak (*turtle* in the Algonquian language) is issuing status cards, claiming they are "a legitimate Aboriginal" group. As I write this, the Canadian literary status quo has been shaken by several debates and events related to Indigenous identity, appropriation and silencing. And in 2016, after the Liberal government announced its commitment to nation-to-nation reconciliation with the Métis Nation, my sister's acquaintance joined many thinking of applying for a Métis card, saying, "Now I can get discounts."

Identity as commodity: lately, researchers and writers have rightly been taken to task for practices that assume stories, myths, artifacts and symbols are theirs to use and to sell, like Disney gift-shop wares, or "food, fun, fashion" cultural samplers.

It's unclear why people choose to pass as a member of another group. Do they find the notion romantic, a way to hearken back to an idealized past? Are they mining cultural goodies they can't acquire as easily in mainstream "white" culture? Or do they want it both ways: the agency and the option of maintaining their legacy of privilege, along with any distinctiveness they might accrue claiming to be a member of a traditionally marginalized group.

(Or is it the discounts? If so, they're in for a surprise.)

I cannot presume to know others' motives, nor to comment on another's identify. I am, however, responsible for trying to understand my own.

Who am I?

I descend largely from settler colonials, and yet I have several Cree and Métis foremothers and forefathers. As a member of a not-uncommon Midwestern Canadian ancestral blend (including Swampy Cree [*maskêkowininiwak/ininiwak*], Métis, French, Irish, Scottish, Danish), I've had plenty of exposure to the contributions and stories of the French, Irish and Scots in school and in the wider culture. What I lack is an understanding of my Indigenous ancestors' lives and stories.

Who am I to tell these stories?

I have never been a member of an Indigenous community whose traditions could be handed down to my siblings and me. Yet Red River historian Norma Hall, who has researched identity issues, argues it's not uncommon for people in this country to grow up unaware of their Indigenous past; further, she says, once they do know, they don't know how to name their identity.

Gregory Scofield writes in an email: "We needn't grow up in that history or knowledge; we simply need to learn and honour it. Claim it."

Do I wish I had been raised to identify as Métis? To be a part of a community that claims me? Of course. But the more deeply I research Red River history, the more profoundly I understand how the entitlement of my settler upbringing has insulated me from the legacy of a past I haven't acknowledged until now. And how little I know. As of this writing, Canada celebrates one hundred and fifty years of Confederation, and I am pierced with an understanding of the reasons many in this country choose not to celebrate.

Colonial settler hand-wringing is not helpful, nor is a longing for innocence. I'm not innocent, but I am curious, unwittingly and sometimes knowingly ignorant, and, as a result, determined to learn more about women in my past who've been ignored, and whose voices have been muted or silenced altogether. To learn, I must first listen, try to see behind the white colonial characterizations of Indigenous women.

Louise Bernice Halfe (Sky Dancer) and I have spent time on the Saskatchewan prairie talking about the lives of women. A celebrated Cree poet whose searing, beautiful language enters troubled spaces, Sky Dancer knows intimately the profound effects of colonialism on women and children. I told Louise what little I knew of my great-grandmother's death and how Catherine Kennedy's story led me to other stories.

"You are honouring the bloodline of your ancestors," Louise told me. Even though, as she says, their "blood runs thin" in me, I am, nonetheless, an inheritor. The call I feel from the past – from Red River up to Hudson Bay – is "an umbilical cord, however slender," connecting me to women whose alliances with fur traders have ultimately – and from a great distance – brought me here now. They are part of me. And, as Gregory Scofield reminds me, when I claim the past, I am claiming those grandmothers, "their lives and histories, their names and the shared blood running through [my] veins."

For good or ill, I owe who I am to those who have gone before – settler and Indigenous both.

In my past are settler relatives who fought against Riel and who were Indian agents, as well as Ininiwak and Métis relatives who were guides, tripmen, hunters, productive and tenacious mothers and active contributors to Red River and Hudson's Bay Company society. It would seem I am a walking contradiction, yet in the messy and shadowy history of this country, I am not. The complicated nature of my mixed identities is testament to this.

Identity cuts to the core of much of the work here. Who was Catherine Kennedy, and who were her foremothers? What did being "half-breed" mean for women in Red River? With no pen and no voice and with their own descendants gone, how can they be known? I hope by reaching back and pulling forward what has been documented about my kin and their contemporaries, I can begin to make them newly visible. Virtually no Red River history is penned by these women, nor is history free from colonial biases; therefore, I must try to see behind the stories – a daunting task. Claiming my heritage in all its contradictions is a step toward understanding my own identity, but first I must learn about the past.

I am looking only at the surface of a long, deep and often unfathomable river of kinship and story running into an even more unfathomable body of water. In this way, I am reminded of Jean Rhys' comment comparing writers' work to rivers that flow into a larger lake. "I don't matter," she says. "The lake matters."

Passages Northwest

*Whichever road I follow, I walk in the land of many gods, and they love
and eat one another…. Suddenly all my ancestors are behind me. Be still,
they say. Watch and listen. You are the result of the love of thousands.*
– Linda Hogan, *Dwellings: A Spiritual History of the Living World*

The long-ago sky: Rupert's Land; the Company on the Bay.
One warm line along rivers. Names she never knew.

"Of course we are," says one aunt.
"Your father's half-breed family," hisses her mother. No stories, no way
to know.

*On a Nova Scotia beach, a curved piece of blue pottery, the size of a shell.
A shipwreck, perhaps? She is drawn to the edge of the water, lost in the past,
asking old questions.*

Another aunt lays her scrapbooks on the table, opens boxes of black-
and-white snaps. "Here's the clipping," says Aunt Kay. "Catherine, the
fire: Warren's Landing. This photo: Her daughters." Three sisters: reti-
cent smiles, coal eyes.

*She walks the edge of the Atlantic among remains of fish traps, ropes.
Blue pottery stamped* Made in England *– a rim here, a handle there.*

What is their provenance? What is hers? Today, the dog walks ahead, sun shakes frost from her bones, unsettles the blood in her veins.

At thirty-two, she climbs into a Hercules heading North to gather Dene workers around a table. Day One: active and passive voice. A raven by the door laughs. She tiptoes from cabin to cabin in the long daylight, her shiny southern shoes sinking in bog and brush. In thirty years, her boots will touch a frozen Northern lake, heavy with awareness, and the sound will crack her open.

She takes the path farther along the shore, thinking water is womb, is graveyard. Tucks another blue shard, smaller, chipped, in her pocket. The ocean brimming with stories.

In Cambridge Bay decades ago, a heap of bones. "Remains of a shaman," says her companion, and the church just over there. So many gods, yet we all die in the wild. A palm reader once held her gaze: "You and an infant fleeing fire," she says, "lost on a northern prairie sea."

Who are her kith, her kin? Bush wives from Severn, Norway House, Red River who raised children, netted snowshoes, dressed furs, comforted company men. Names come in pieces: Ke-che-cho-wick, Wash-e-soo-E'Squew, Mary, Kitty, Sally, Catherine.

After days of north winds, she finds a small midden of blue and white nestled in shale, carries the shards to the house. A bowl? A tureen? The sea, like the past, emptying its pockets of loose change. She rearranges fragments, salt-bone surfaces each to each, testing fit.

In Between

These anecdotes and descriptions of women in Red River and Northern Manitoba communities reveal the ways their mixed descent made them "other" in the eyes of many – not *this*, not *that*, eluding definition, except where Canada (or, earlier, the Hudson's Bay Company or the Queen) presumed to define them. They were not white enough or "Indian" enough, not Christian or the right kind of Christian, not "respectably" married.

Like most women, the nineteenth-century Red River women portrayed here lived porous and fluid lives with overlapping identities, their many names and roles as imprisoning as they were freeing.

Today, legions of women in the Indigenous diaspora are far removed from the root communities that bore them generations ago. Yet the land can itself be considered the root community. Bev Sellars reminds us that Indigenous people "do not have a homeland to which we can return. This is our homeland and we are not going anywhere."

Home to me is difficult to define. I am most at ease near an open horizon – the sea or the prairie – and in a natural environment. Does my DNA stir in that landscape, recalling pre-contact Hudson Bay, the openness of Lake Winnipeg, the Prairies, the cliffs of Ireland or islands off the coast of Scotland? Molecular scientists suggest our trans-genetic memories survive generations. Or is the pull simply a wish I share with many – to pare life to the essentials.

A shoreline, a riverbank, a threshold, an edge – in between.

Traces

Mixed-descent Red River women of the nineteenth century were found in all social classes, yet details about ordinary people are sparse and inconsistent. Census records can be unreliable – people forgot (or changed) their birthdate, refused to name their father, renounced their church, included friends and orphans in the household, changed their preferred name from one census to another or, perhaps attempting to be helpful, gave the enumerator who came to the village approximate details of their absent neighbour's family.

When Métis filmmaker Christine Welsh searched for information about her great-great-grandmother Margaret Taylor (country wife of Governor George Simpson) she was unable to find a written record: "her voice is not heard in the historical record..." The code of silence in Welsh's family was a "thick web of denial, shame, bitterness, and silence." In my family, the silence had less effort behind it; it was more insidious. We ignored Natives on the streets of The Pas or Saskatoon or Winnipeg, and my parents ignored my father's roots. Later, my mother used his background as an epithet of disgust when their marriage began to fail.

We don't see you. We don't talk about you. We keep no record of your lives.

This code of silence makes gathering information difficult. When I broadened my search beyond my family, I found accounts of women in the fur trade were written almost exclusively by HBC factors, traders, the clergy and adventurers – all European men. Scouring nineteenth-century publications for mentions of women (using a variety of search terms), I often came up empty – not a single anecdote about any female, European or Indigenous.

When there are historical records, we tend to listen primarily to the ones we consider palatable, largely Anglo-European authors and journal-keepers. As novelist Fred Stenson says, "We have looked the group of witnesses over, and have listened only to the 'credible ones': meaning the white ones, the literate ones, the ones in positions of power."

But ordinary Red River women were there, are still here, in the liminal spaces that resonate in old journals, the lacunae of history. They embody the in between.

Years of searching took me to Library and Archives Canada in Ottawa, to the Hudson's Bay Company Archives Library of Manitoba, to the Diocese of Rupert's Land, to regional Manitoba libraries and to old bookshops. I scoured both online and offline materials (newsletters, community histories), walked the land, held interviews and conversations and took road trips around Winnipeg and farther north. Soon, I began to find the occasional incomplete anecdote, and the rare story in which the woman was central. Not surprisingly, many Red River stories that survived involve sex scandals and Alice Munro–like challenges to legitimacy: "who do you think you are?" I bring these stories of "half-breed" women forward so their details don't remain in old records, so they live now in the present, where they can teach us.

The search has been worth every haystack, lost needle, road trip and conversation; every dark afternoon winding a screeching lever on a microfilm reader; every hard-won shred of testimony scoured from an almost unreadable diary or musty, century-old book. There is no whole story to tell of any of these women, but as I continued to dig, the search would uncover a past both sobering and humbling. I would find cousins I didn't know I had, create nourishing friendships and nurture a longing to know more about the past.

Red River women are introduced here in scraps, found poems, historical snippets, narrative snapshots, shards of memory and the occasional image – assembled and organized largely chronologically around the lifetimes of my own Indigenous and "half-breed" ancestors. The incomplete pieces here are markers, signposts of a larger history we need to re-examine and preserve.

Names

In Rupert's Land, many words were used for mixed-descent women, including "half-breed" and "commodity." At the time, white European women were often referred to as "the sex" or "exotics." "Country-born," a term coined in the twentieth century by John Elgin Foster, has been used to refer to an Anglo-Native blend (of Cree and Scot, for example). Today, the term "Métis" is understood to refer to a distinct group of Indigenous people whose identity was first forged in the historic Red River Settlement, not simply a catch-all synonym for "mixed race."

I have used the terms "mixed-ancestry," "mixed-blood" and "mixed descent," particularly when the terms were in use at the time. I have avoided "mixed race" because I find the concepts of "pure" and "mixed" race problematic; race is a cultural construct, spurious and, I'd argue, not a legitimate concept to begin with. Ta-Nehisi Coates's words echo my thoughts: "...race is the child of racism, not the father. And the process of naming 'the people' has never been a matter of genealogy and physiognomy so much as one of hierarchy."

In the eighteenth- and nineteenth-century fur trade, the term "half-breed" (often written "Half Breed") was common. Perhaps the word was considered more literal then: a newly arrived York Factory Scot in the eighteenth century takes an Ininiwak "bush" wife and they have a "half-breed" child. Since then, the word has been used widely regardless of the blend of European and Indigenous ancestry, despite the post–Riel Rebellion rise of the word *Métis* to refer to a member of that distinct group. While it's true each of us is a blend of cultures and backgrounds, the issue of naming Indigenous identities is complicated by the often confusing and tangled categories established by governments and the church. There are many ways to take the Indian out of the child, and many names to move the process along.

Following the River

I have used terms such as "half-breed" or "Indian" when I am quoting a source who uses them, when I am emphasizing discrimination or when I am assuming the attitude of such a source during that time. "Half-breed" is typically associated with government records. While I understand the term "Native" can be problematic, it seems to carry less official baggage, is more informal and – in my limited experience – seems commonly used within Indigenous communities. As well, "Native" or "Native-born" were terms my Red River ancestors would have used in the nineteenth century.

Red River genealogy is known for the swirl of variations in given names and their invented spellings. My relations are no exception. The census taker wrote Asmas instead of Erasmus, for example. The names Kate, Catie (Katie), Kit, Kay, Catherine (Catharine), Kitty, Eleanore, Antoine (Antwain, Anthony), Sarah and Sally were repeated, borrowed or adopted within families and across generations. In Fort Alexander, Catherine Kennedy used the name Suzan on the birth record of her eldest child.

In found material, I have kept the source's original spelling, and have not always used *sic* to indicate this. A list of the characters in my past is found in the appendix.

Hearing the Music

Did you ever go into an Irishman's shanty
where money was scarce and whiskey aplenty,
a three-legged stool, a table, a match,
a door and a handle without any latch.
– "Irishman's Shanty" (traditional song)

My father sang it before I understood it. "It's my Irish side," he'd say, and on St. Paddy's Day, he'd urge us to find something green to wear, even if it was a piece of paper pinned on our shirts, cut in the shape of a shamrock. We had little money, but one year my mother found a way to fashion a kilt – likely not her family's Scottish tartan, but plaid nonetheless – and off I went to highland dance lessons in someone's living room in a small northern Alberta town along the CNR line.

I preferred tap, though; it recalled the era of grand musicals on film, and I loved the sound of the metal at the toe, its clippity-clop on the linoleum as I stumbled through basic steps, remnants of which I'd resurrect for years ahead whenever I had the opportunity to dance.

God, I have loved to dance.

And, of course, *Frère Jacques, frère Jacques, dormez-vous, dormez-vous* – what child of the '50s or '60s wasn't fed that song in a round, a musical game to keep us busy at birthday parties, around campfires. "Our French side," said my father.

Songs and dances were a world as small as I was. My relatives were all over the country – each of us in our sealed-off families, moving from one town to the next, pursuing the postwar dream of – what? Progress, they called it. Aunts, several cousins, a French uncle, a Scottish grandmother, a gruff Irish American grandfather who died when I was still too young to form questions.

About kin, about community.

But then I wasn't anymore – young, that is – and Eleanore, my prairie grandmother, the tall, quiet woman who adored my father – her only boy – was still an enigma. Her commanding air left me awestruck. Her long white hair was held up by combs, and she'd brush it out each night in a room overlooking her extravagant prairie garden. Abundant fresh vegetables ready for steaming and canning, fat blooms of flowers lolling in the Saskatchewan sun. In each visit, undercurrents: her reticence and firm faith, my mother's resentment. I knew Jesus from Sunday school – he loves me, this I know; pages to colour; tiny envelopes for a quarter or a dime. *Anglican, Catholic, Presbyterian* were words, not weapons.

How do we know who we are as children? Our eager eyes and ears take in habits, superstition, clothing, school lessons, newspapers. Read the world, listen for its direction and then learn to focus, repeat what we've heard. Stay comfortable. Absence isn't yet presence in a young mind. I did not know what I didn't know – about God or skin colour or the other side of the tracks, how truisms become bromides, where lines are drawn.

But they're drawn. Eleanore was silent about her Red River roots. Not a word about her mother's death – did the trauma bury them? Did Catherine teach her daughter Eleanore to speak nêhiyawêwin or bungi? Michif? Did the first words on her tongue become a whisper, then disappear into the air?

We are spun creatures, wrapped in custom and intention, and we carry memories of a tune, a piece of clothing, a dance into the beating heart of a new day, composing our own music as we go.

Eleanore, what if Catherine had passed along stories for you to pass along to us? Would my sister and brothers and I feel – what? – whole? Rooted? Connected by more than the string of railway houses across the Prairies – Edson, Prince Albert, Saskatoon, Thunder Bay, Dauphin, The Pas? What if I had been curious sooner?

When memories shred over time like fragile silk, and tenuous strands of kinship fly off in a rough wind, what becomes of the music? Is there a fiddle or a pipe to gather notes from the wavering air, send them across distant waters, sing us home?

Part One: Setting Out

Driving North

It's twenty below and the wind is fierce. I am held inside Aunt Kay's hand-me-down fur coat, the warmest piece of clothing I own. When I wear it, I find myself looking over my shoulder for an anti-fur activist armed with a pail of paint.

"My aunt gave it to me," I'll say. "Do you want me to toss it in a landfill?"

And besides, where I'm going has its roots in the fur trade. It's also small-town Canada, my favourite destination. I begin my search for details of my great-grandmother Catherine Kennedy's story with a trip to Selkirk, where Catherine lived and raised her children, one of whom is my grandmother Eleanore.

My goal for this trip: to find the dock in Selkirk where the lake steamer SS *Premier* set out. And to find Taylor Avenue. Tucked in my backpack is a photo of Catherine and Eleanore standing outside their house.

I take Henderson Highway out of Winnipeg, following the Red River on my left. Its name has been almost mythical since I was a child. La rivière Rouge. Du nord. River of Blood. It is over eight hundred kilometres long, about two hundred and fifty of those in Canada. River of folk song and North American history, it is the waterway you follow downstream to the mouth of Lake Winnipeg, and from there farther north to the Nelson River and north again to Hudson Bay. The river for which the Red River Settlement is named, despite the fact the colony itself stretched far west and north from its waters. I am in Treaty 1 territory.

And recently, Red River of tragic news. Of Tina Fontaine and other missing or murdered women whose bodies are found in its waters or along its shores. Of dedicated searchers known as Drag the Red. The river of tears.

The grit of this knowledge settles in as I pass the grand homes along Henderson Highway. A few '40s- and '50s-era houses, as well as one with the sharp angles of a Frank Lloyd Wright structure. Once an area of expensive, gracious country homes separate from urban frenzy, the community is now an extension of Winnipeg. Here and there are clusters of new-builds with the distinctive stone grey of Western suburban creep.

Although I lived in Manitoba for many years, I don't recall visiting Selkirk, nor did I make the pilgrimage to Skinner's in Lockport for their famous hot dogs. My husband often took my mother to Skinner's when he was in Winnipeg visiting his own family. I have photos Allan took of Mom in one of the '50s-diner-style booths, and a few of her overlooking the Red River, wearing her dark glasses, a jaunty boater and a blue plaid jacket. She was an irascible and difficult mother-in-law, yet during her last years the two of them had reached a truce. Did she know how deeply my father's roots were planted along this river? I didn't.

The Silver Chief. That's the name Saulteaux (Ojibwe) and Cree people gave Thomas Douglas, Lord Selkirk, two centuries ago. My father, who worked on the railway, was often called the Silver Fox, for reasons, I'm sure, far different from those that earned Lord Selkirk his nickname. A cynical mind might draw a slim analogy between the two men, one legendary in Western Canadian settler history, another completely unknown: both believed their actions were triumphant, important, yet both – depending on whom you ask – left a path of destruction in their wake.

The poet Robbie Burns knew the young Thomas Douglas well. Burns had no use for a "birkie, ca'd a lord," yet he was a staunch friend of Lord Selkirk's family, the Douglases. As a young man, Thomas Douglas went to school in Edinburgh with Sir Walter Scott. You have to hand it to Selkirk: an ear for poetry, a head for business, a heart to save Scottish crofters from starvation and an eye for a patch of land across the Atlantic larger than the whole of the United Kingdom.

My lens is wide open as I drive. Time slows. I look back and forth along the road for signs, anything familiar from the histories I've been reading. Who camped under those trees? Could Catherine or her mother, Sally, have walked here? Catherine's father, Antoine Kennedy? Members of the Peguis Nation, surely. I must have kin who travelled along the river in a cart or a wagon or a barge, who fished from these banks.

St. Clements and St. Andrews come alive in Red River settler history, but visible only through a windshield, they seem, well, pleasant but ordinary. Had I hoped for an old stone foundation, a palimpsest, traces – after hundreds of seasons – of the original settlement peeking through? The only established historic site nearby seems to be Lower Fort Garry, and it's closed for the season.

Imagining from the comfort of a warm car is, of course, a luxury and a romantic indulgence. But then again, from the mindset of a nineteenth-century Scot – *Rich resources! Adventure! New beginnings!* – expansion in the "New" World was a romantic notion too.

Selkirk saw opportunity in this territory, and for several years attempted to establish settlements in what so many thought of as virginal land, ripe for civilizing. In 1808, he saw his chance. The Napoleonic Wars affected stocks in the London-based Hudson's Bay Company (HBC), and Selkirk bought enough shares to give him a say in the business. Fur traders would soon be retiring, settlements in the New World needed local agriculture – shipping food from the Old World or Upper Canada was expensive – and the Red River Valley was a prime location to relocate Scots who were victims of the High-land Clearances, eager to flee straths where their houses were burned behind them. Selkirk received a land grant of over 250,000 square kilometres from HBC and assembled 120 men to make the trip to the New World.

There was a problem, however. The group was to settle at the inter-section of the Red and the Assiniboine Rivers, right on the North West Company's (NWC's) main trade route. The Hudson's Bay Company and the NWC were already at odds and would soon be at war. Settle-ment would only add fuel to the fire, especially if the settlers and their leader, Selkirk, pursued their cockamamie goal of farming.

Roderick MacBeth, whose father was among the first Scottish settlers, described Lord Selkirk as a man of "singular unselfishness, striving to ameliorate wrong conditions and staunch the wounds of the world." Others called him the Apostle of Western Colonization. He was providing the Scots with a home where "tyrannous landlord-ism would have no place."

Apostle or not, Lord Selkirk clashed with the NWC, and blood was shed at the Battle of Seven Oaks, a significant event in the birth of the Métis nation. Selkirk seized the main post at Fort William, and the North West Company took him to court. His wealth evaporated in court costs and he returned to England, then to Pau, France, where he died of consumption at forty-nine. Selkirk hasn't really left, however; his name lives on in the City of Selkirk, on several street signs across Manitoba and as far away as British Columbia, on an Ontario park and on several Canadian schools, hotels and community centres.

The wind shakes the car. Here's a time to wonder about the labourers, outdoors all day drying fish or in camps making clothes or pound-ing pemmican: workers indentured to the Hudson's Bay Company or, before the 1821 merger, to its competitor, the North West Company. What did ordinary people know of Selkirk and his grand plan? I have found few accounts of the lives of common white settlers or Natives alike – those who built boats, lived in makeshift tents, scrabbled under snow for frozen root crops to stay alive.

I pass Skinner's restaurant, drive across the river and in a few kilometres come to the outskirts of the town of Selkirk. This is the place where Catherine raised eleven children. She was born on Eveline Street, according to Aunt Kay – and then moved to Taylor Avenue. This doesn't jibe with records showing her birth family living on one of the St. Peter's Reserve lots farther downriver, but I hope to sort that out. I park at the edge of town and pull out the photo of Catherine and Eleanore outside a simple white wooden house.

If I find the house, it will be something tangible. Catherine Kennedy Couture, Red River woman whose death is family lore, but whose life is largely a mystery.

First, I need to orient myself. I drive down Main Street and around the town to get my bearings. There's Eveline Street – it follows along the Red – and what looks like the main wharf. Next to it, an iron sculpture of men in a York boat, the legendary mode of travel on inland waterways during the days of the fur trade.

When I open the car door a crack, the fierce wind whips it wide open. I manage to snap a photo before retreating into the car. Is this the wharf? A few blocks from downtown I spy a lighthouse and three vessels next to a waterside park. The SS *Keenora* looks a lot like what the SS *Premier* would have looked like. Both steamboats. The *Keenora* served as a floating dance hall in Winnipeg before it was put into service on Manitoba waterways.

Is this where Catherine boarded each time she travelled north to visit her husband, Antoine? Or did she visit only the once?

Where the road turns into Taylor Avenue, I see the rusty hulk of an old ship in shallow and weedy water, a south-running channel of the Red. At the corner is a stately old tawny brick house, its windows boarded up. Was the house here when Catherine lived down the street?

Following the River

Nothing on Taylor Avenue looks like the little white house in the photo. Nothing. Taylor is a short street on the east side of the tracks, and every house looks to be no older than sixty or seventy years. Are there archival photos of the street to be found?

Driving along Manitoba Avenue, I pass the legendary Manitoba Asylum, now the Selkirk Mental Health Centre; "gone to Selkirk" was a pejorative term for mental illness when I was growing up. I turn into the parking lot of the new public library, pull on my backpack and hunch toward the door in Aunt Kay's coat, determined to find information about Selkirk families, including the Coutures and, if possible, Catherine's parents, the Kennedys. The wind is bitter and bites at my face.

Crossing Waters:
Notes and Recollections

The maps spread out on my table in Nova Scotia are a jumble – a newer map of Manitoba, veined with roads and waterways; an old hand-drawn map of the Red River area from the junction of the Red and the Assiniboine, north to what is now called Selkirk; and a map of Rupert's Land, that vast area below and around Hudson Bay the HBC claimed as its own for over two hundred years. The Red, Nelson and Hayes Rivers drain northward into Hudson Bay.

The size of Canada's North never ceases to amaze me. Northerners tell me they wouldn't move south and give up the openness and quiet, the flora and fauna. Yet in the last few decades, Canada's North has become a climate coal-mine canary and, increasingly, the site of our country's shame, the unrelenting devastation of Indigenous peoples.

Looking at Northern Manitoba, I try to imagine the landscape from above, its moving trails of water pulled steadily into the larger body, then flowing farther eastward and out to sea. Generations before the railway reached Winnipeg in the 1880s, these water routes were used for transport between Europe and this land. And for thousands of years before that, Cree and other Indigenous peoples had navigated the waterways of the region.

Out the window, I see a fishing boat headed back from its early morning run. Every year, we hear of another loss on the water; the Atlantic is unforgiving.

As was travel in Rupert's Land. If my measurements are accurate, the distance from the Red River area to York Factory is over fifteen hundred kilometres. People travelled this distance burdened with heavy goods, portaging when necessary, camping in every imaginable condition.

I gather notes about York boats, Red River carts and my own memories.

York Factory, circa 1820

The first York boats, based on Orkney whaling boats, began to replace canoes as the primary form of transport between Red River and York Factory and throughout the HBC northern district. Six to ten men worked their twenty-foot oars often sixteen hours a day to move up to three tons of cargo.

In open water, a sail eased the trip. In shallow water and on land, tripmen rolled the boat over logs and used poles to inch the boat from one open waterway to another. Sometimes, when they had to travel against the current, they'd walk along the shore and drag the boats using tumplines, straps around their heads allowing them to use their spines rather than their shoulders to bear the weight.

Red River, 1860
from the *Nor'wester*, Thursday, June 14, 1860

Boats off to York Factory
The first week of this month was a busy one for those who freight from York Factory, Hudson's Bay. The boats nearly all left then. Although there may have been about three dozen – a large proportion of them belonging to the HBC – these so-called "boats" are open barges of about 30 feet in length with a carrying capacity of 4 or 5 tonne…they are primitive-looking crafts when brought side to side with the Anson Northrup. They

will be back with heavy cargoes in the end of July. Between 1500 and 1600 bales of furs, collected within the Red River district, have been set off by the boats for England.

Red River, 1862

from the *Nor'wester*, September 11, 1862

To the Editors of the Nor'Wester
Gentlemen: The frequent delays in the steamboat freight business and the successful competition carried on for the past two years by Harris and Whiteford's barge scheme have suggested to me another method of freighting between St. Paul and Red River Settlement.... Let a small company be formed that will run York boats between this and George-town [HBC post in what is now Minnesota], *and have a train of Red River carts constantly moving between Georgetown and St. Cloud or St. Paul – all to be worked by Red River hands. I am sometimes surprised that some of the old freighters from York Factory do not try their hands at the old business in this new field. Those freighters have boats lying rotting on their banks, and what is still better, they understand the business thoroughly from their long experience.... One great advantage they would have is they could get men very easily. There are always dozens lying about the Fort, lounging and skulking, too lazy for farm labor, but fond of tripping, especially if the distance is not very great. Then, again, the Settlement is swarming with oxen which might find ample employment on the carting part of this scheme. Money is scarce, we are told, and true it is, but here is a way by which money could be saved from leaving the country.*

I remain, Gentlemen
Yours truly
An Old Voyageur

Things to Know about a Red River Cart

1. Made of wood and rawhide. No iron was used.
2. Carried up to 1200 pounds of goods, furs, supplies.
3. Its high-axle wheels, wide and rounded, moved over land easily.
4. Was pulled by any strong animal, usually oxen.
5. Wheels, when removed, could be wrapped in hides for flotation, allowing the cart to serve as a barge.
6. Workings were never greased; dust gathered, causing ear-splitting screeches as carts passed by.
7. Steamboats and the railway were death knells for the Red River cart.
8. Hundreds of carts filled Red River Colony roadways well into the 1860s. Today, you can count on one hand the number of carts left – one is at Lower Fort Garry.

Lake Winnipeg, August 1906
Still all my song shall be nearer, my God, to Thee.

She was the pride of Lake Winnipeg. Named for the fourth daughter of Queen Victoria, the SS *Princess* was equipped with side paddles, reminiscent of the legendary Mississippi steamers. A ship's version of Princess Leia's side buns.

The *Princess* was christened in 1881, when the royal she was named for, Princess Louise Caroline Alberta, would have been in her thirties. Queen Victoria's fourth daughter was a rebel – gossip was rampant about her habits of smoking, riding a bicycle, sculpting and writing newspaper articles under a pseudonym. She entered a loveless marriage with a subject of the Crown rumoured to be homosexual. That man, John Campbell, was the Duke of Argyll, Marquess of Lorne, and became the fourth Governor General of Canada in 1878. The District of Alberta (now part of the Province of Alberta) was named for Louise.

In 1881, when the paddleboat *Princess* was christened, Catherine Kennedy would have been married to Antoine Couture for about five years. If she were a reader, she may have known about the notorious Princess Louise, but more likely she'd have heard about the steamer, the most splendid lake vessel of her time. Those side paddles allowed the *Princess* to travel at twenty-five knots, about half the highway speed of cars today. Her forty-passenger cabins were stylish and luxurious.

In a few short years, however, the SS *Princess*'s heyday was over.

In March of 1885, over one thousand kilometres away from Lake Winnipeg, Métis occupied Duck Lake, Saskatchewan, the first of many battles in which Métis resisted Canadian expansion. Twice as many North-West Mounted Police died as Métis; the first Métis to die, however, was Isidore Dumont, Métis leader Gabriel Dumont's brother. In May, several days after the Battle of Batoche, Louis Riel surrendered.

Later, when a thousand soldiers were transported from Grand Rapids on the west side of the lake, the SS *Princess* was one of the vessels to return them to Winnipeg. That same year, she was gutted and downgraded. The property of the North West Navigation Company of Winnipeg, the pride of the lake, the SS *Princess* became a workhorse.

For another twenty-five years, the once-glamorous *Princess* towed barges, carried heavy goods such as railway ties and hauled a bounty of millions of tons of fish from one end of Lake Winnipeg to the other.

By 1906, Catherine and Antoine Couture had eleven children. Antoine worked at Warren's Landing at the top of Lake Winnipeg with two or three of their adult children, while Catherine raised the others at their home on Taylor Avenue in Selkirk.

A short distance away from them, on Eveline Street, lived Master Mariner John Hawes and his wife, Mary – English settlers who, in a few short years, filled their house with six children, one of whom, Dorothea, was around the same age as Catherine's daughter Nettie.

Hawes was now captain of the SS *Princess*. In late August, he set out on Lake Winnipeg, along with other Selkirk residents, including seventeen-year-old Flora McDonald, the cabin servant, and nineteen-year-old Johanna Palsdottir, a cook. Below, the cargo hold included sixteen hundred boxes of fish. The *Princess* had left the Spider Islands, south of Norway House and Warren's Landing, and was headed south toward Little George Island.

About suppertime the evening of August 25, 1906, a powerful northeast wind rose. The ship had rounded Little George Island, and the force of the growing storm caused Captain Hawes to rethink his decision to continue south to Swampy Island (now called Berens Island). The *Princess* was taking on water.

The waves on the lake rose to eight metres, and Captain Hawes ordered full speed back to Little George.

Suddenly, the hull split apart, trapping crew below and extinguishing the ship's fires. The engines of the *Princess* stopped.

Fourteen people on board escaped in two boats. One of them, Mrs. Sinclair, held her eight-month-old baby under one arm as she bailed water out of the yawl with the other. Her husband chopped at the tackle with an axe, trying to release the yawl.

Captain Hawes and young Flora and Johanna held to the sinking wreck.

"The girls wouldn't leave," Fireman George Freeman said later. "I tried to pull Flora McDonald across the cabin roof, but she said, 'I am safe with the captain.' Then the women began to sing 'Nearer My God to Thee.' Such a heart-rending scene I have never before witnessed. The waves swept around the captain and the girls, and still their song was heard."

The two small boats – yawl and lifeboat – made it to Swampy Island by early morning.

Only two bodies were ever found, one of which was the captain's. All that was left on his body were the straps of his life preserver.

Winnipeg, circa 1960

She'd purse her lips into a big smooch.

Then: a tube of bright red lipstick – two straight lines, one across the top lip, one across the bottom – her smile, opening into a red zig-zagged line, a fan unfolding.

My mother's mother was a widow who doted on her grandchildren; a meal at the Paddlewheel was Gram's birthday treat, and it meant our best clothes. She counted out the dollars and cents from her pension, closed her handbag with a snap and put on her Persian lamb, a wearable carpet of black and shiny tight curls.

The elevator operator at The Bay opened the scissor-gate doors, and we walked past the replica of a large paddlewheel, a grand display with running water. Above, a ceiling painted in steam clouds, and on the walls, a photograph or two of Red River carts. I'd scan the glass shelves in the cafeteria line – cubed Jell-O with whipped cream, aspic salad, roast pork or beef – mull over my options and order the fish and chips. Fresh fish was exotic to me; I was used to fish sticks out of a box. On rare occasions, a neighbour brought home a pickerel from a fishing trip, but most food in our house began life walking around a farm.

Back then, I was concerned only with a Saturday outing and the crisp battered fish on my plate. The history of boats on Lake Winnipeg? Not a clue. I always knew the Hudson's Bay Company was about the fur trade – maybe not those Persian lambs – but to me, The Bay was the architectural grande dame on Portage, a couple of blocks west of its competitor, Eaton's. You were either an Eaton's person or a Bay person, and we were the latter. When Gram took me there, it was a chance to see, in my dad's words, "how the other half lives."

What did I know?

Decades later, and Gram and my parents are gone. I live on the East Coast, grateful for fresh fish. I now know ancestors of mine worked for the three-hundred-and-fifty-year-old company that once claimed fifteen percent of the North American land mass: colonialism at its finest. Poet Garry Thomas Morse writes about one of my forebears, Matthew Cocking, who likely thought "the sun would never set on HBC." At this writing, the building that once housed the Paddlewheel Restaurant has closed all floors but two, and its future as a brick-and-mortar company is uncertain. HBC has moved online.

Today, fish stocks on Lake Winnipeg are a tiny percentage of what they were a century ago. The legendary York boat is used only for regattas and historical displays. Steamboats no longer carry tourists and heavy cargo to Norway House. In fact, they no longer travel on Lake Winnipeg at all.

Winnipeg, 2015

My sister and I drive down Portage Avenue, make a turn into the parkade behind The Bay, walk across St. Mary Avenue and climb the stone steps of the Archives of Manitoba to look for clues. We talk about the Paddlewheel, Gram and her Persian lamb coat. I find out karakul lambs are killed before they are three days old to preserve the shiny black colour of the fur and ensure the most lucrative profit. There's a metaphor in there somewhere.

Later, after a search through microfiche, I return to the room where my sister is at a terminal scrolling through information.

"Almost done," Allison says. I pick up the familiar piece of paper on the desk and hand it to her.

"Don't forget this."

"That's yours," she says. "I thought it was yours, anyway. It was here when I sat down."

"But I wasn't working here."

It's a photocopy of a two-page spread from the St. Michael's church history, one page announcing the funerals in Selkirk for Catherine

Kennedy and a young boy, Augustus Weil. On the following page is the photo of Catherine outside the house on Taylor Avenue with Eleanore, our grandmother, beside her. The same one I used the winter before to try to locate the house in Selkirk.

The same still tucked in my backpack. I pull it out.

We look at each other.

Allison's brown eyes widen. I love it – reminds me of the curious little girl I remember.

At the desk, the librarian shakes her head in disbelief. "People look for a million different things here," she says. "What are the odds someone else is researching a steamboat disaster in 1908?"

She swivels around. "Oh, I know who. He was just here." She cranes her neck to look beyond the shelves.

"Nope. Gone."

"Do you know who he was?" I ask, knowing full well she can't tell me that.

Later that night, back at Allison's, I stay up late searching online for names of people who might be writing or have already written about Selkirk steamboats, ships, transport, the SS *Premier*. ·

The topic of waterways, river systems and transport north from Red River is larger than I knew.

At this point it seems, well, fathomless.

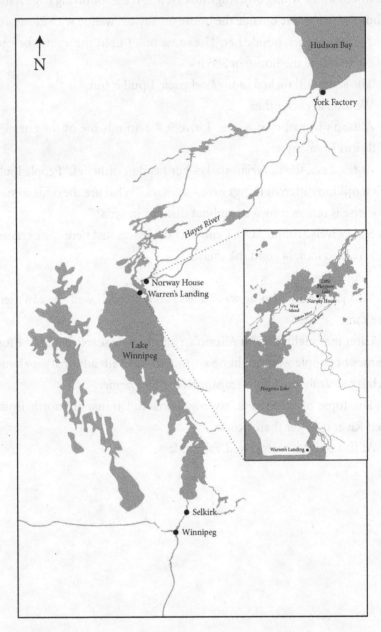

Waters North. Map courtesy of Kathy Kaulbach, Touchstone Design House.

Lost

"Do you know how I might find the Stone Church?" The two women behind the library counter cock their heads and frown.

"The one across the river?" one asks the other.

"Well, with this snow, the road likely isn't open anyway." She offers an apologetic shrug.

Outside the large glass windows, the horizon is flat white. The wind hasn't let up and I'm still disoriented. I have no local knowledge: maybe I'm wrong about the name.

Learning from the page has its limits. The body needs to know.

St. Peter's is key to learning who Catherine and her family were. The church is one of Rupert's Land's oldest, built in 1853. Yet I'm not even sure of its name. St. Peter's? St. Peter Dynevor? The old Anglican church? The Indian church? Old Stone Church? Its name changes with every source. I find a sign that reads St. Peter's, but this church is a white wooden building. Then I become turned around, unsure which direction is north.

I was born and grew up on the Prairies, for heaven's sake. It shouldn't be this easy to get lost.

But I am lost, both in the town and in the past. After months back in Nova Scotia with my nose in nineteenth-century records, I'm dizzy with a swirl of information. My focus is diffuse, and I grab at any detail, hoping it will point me in the right direction. I find a tidbit or clue, only to have it reappear elsewhere as a different date or a slightly different name.

Following the River

After I leave the library, I take another loop around Selkirk and manage to find St. Michael's Cemetery on the outskirts of town. Perhaps I can find Catherine's grave. The wind has blown snow into waves, and the turn-in to the property is ice and gravel.

The gate is locked, but the snowbank against it prevents me from opening it anyway, so I lean over the fence. I'd searched cemeteries online and found a picture of Catherine's gravestone, but the photo had been taken in summer. I look to the left of the field.

There you are, Catherine. I can't make out the inscription, but there you are.

Beside her stone is another, smaller stone. I recall Aunt Kay saying she thought it might be that of an infant child. I'll come back and bring Kay with me. Our memory keeper, Catherine's granddaughter, our link to the past.

I return to the car. Lower Fort Garry is closed, the maritime museum in town is closed, I know no one here. I don't know which end of the river is upstream and which is downstream. The cold has set in, the town stilled in snow and ice. The ghostly moon I saw earlier in the morning is no longer visible.

In the place where many of my people came from, I'm a stranger. And worse, I don't know what I don't know.

"You have a lot of cousins in Selkirk, you know." During one of my visits with Kay in her Winnipeg apartment years ago, I waited, looking at all the bric-a-brac on her walls, as she brought out stacks of albums and scrapbooks with newspaper clippings and photos. Any time I've heard her narrate the stories on the pages, I'm overwhelmed. My mind can't hold all the details. Kay has always wanted to visit her cousins in Selkirk. I'll have to make that happen.

Not in this weather, though. Grateful, at least, for the embrace of Kay's fur coat, I turn up the car heater and feel the wind buffet the vehicle as I head south to Winnipeg.

WHEN I RETURN TO NOVA SCOTIA, I hit the books again. Books, online sources, any resource I can find. I have two hundred years of history to learn.

Chief Peguis granted land to the Church Missionary Society of London, England, to establish a mission at Cooks Creek in Rupert's Land in 1833. Cooks Creek is the north end of what we now know as Selkirk.

St. Peter Dynevor "Old Stone Church" was built as a community effort under the direction of Reverend William Cockran. In May of 1853, its cornerstone was consecrated; members of what was known as the Indian Settlement hauled stone from the river for the walls. Stained glass windows were shipped across the Atlantic, protected in barrels of molasses hardened before shipping and heated to liquid on arrival.

It's a start. Around 1850, several years before Catherine Kennedy was born, close to five hundred residents were living near Cooks Creek on the east side of the Red, north of Sugar Point – in what is now St. Peter's Reserve. The community had cultivated two hundred or more acres, something that must have given Reverend Cockran pleasure. More than anything, William Cockran wanted the wayward Indian souls under his care to learn how to raise crops and animals, to turn away from what he saw as their peripatetic and pagan ways.

The new church was possible, Cockran writes in his journal, because of the money, supplies, labour and food provided by a slew of local families, including Chief Peguis's family, the Cooks, the Fletts, the Kennedys, the Sinclairs, the Spences and others.

To know one of my relatives may have hauled stone from the Red, carried those windows, hammered nails, and to know his wife, Sally (Sarah), and one of his older daughters may have provided food during the years of construction – this is the first stirring I feel of connection.

It's the body again, the ache for the physical, the material our forebears may have touched.

I will find the church. Perhaps a grave.

Peguis: A Final Bargain

Chief Peguis (1774–1864), also known as Cut-Nose, migrant to Red River, Saulteaux leader "St. Peter's Band," baptized William King.

Letter to the Aborigines' Protection Society,
London, England 1857

Many winters ago, in 1812, the lands along the Red River, in the Assinniboine country on which I and the tribe of Indians of whom I am chief then lived, were taken possession of, without permission of myself or my tribe, by a body of white settlers.

For the sake of peace, I, as the representative of my tribe, allowed them to remain on our lands on their promising that we should be well paid for them by a great chief, who was to follow them. This great chief, whom we call the Silver Chief (the Earl of Selkirk), arrived in the spring after the war between the North West and Hudson's Bay Companies (1817).

He told us he wanted land for some of his countrymen, who were very poor in their own country; and I consented, on the condition that he paid well for my tribe's land, he could have from the confluence of the Assinniboine to near Maple Sugar Point on the Red River (a distance of twenty to twenty-four miles), following the course of the river, and as far back on each side of the river as a horse could be seen under (easily distinguished).

The Silver Chief told us he had little with which to pay us for our lands when he made this arrangement, in consequence of the troubles of the North-west Company. He, however, asked us what we most required for the present, and we told him we would be content till the following year, when he promised again to return, to take only ammunition and tobacco. The Silver Chief never returned, and either his son or the Hudson's Bay Company have ever since paid us annually for our lands only the small quantity of ammunition and tobacco which in the first instance we took as a preliminary to a final bargain about our lands.

Three–Dollar Bill

— and all Indians inhabiting the district — do hereby
cede, release, surrender and yield up to Her Majesty the
Queen and successors forever all the lands — Beginning at
the international boundary line — at a point due north
— thence to run due north to the centre — thence northward
to the centre — thence by the middle of the lake and the middle
of the river — thence by the River to its mouth — westwardly,
including all the islands — thence westwardly to a point
— thence in a straight line to the crossing of the rapids
— thence due south — and thence eastwardly by the said line

to the place of beginning.

— To have and to hold the same to Her said Majesty the Queen
and Her successors forever — to lay aside and reserve for the sole
and exclusive use of the Indians — so much of land on both sides of
the Red River, beginning at the south line of St. Peter's Parish — one
hundred and sixty acres for each family of five — it being understood,
however, that if there are any settlers within the bounds of any lands
reserved by any band, Her Majesty reserves the right to deal with
such settlers as She shall deem just.

– And with a view to show the satisfaction of Her Majesty
with the behaviour and good conduct of Her Indians, parties
to this treaty, She hereby – makes them a present of three dollars for
each Indian man, woman and child –

(Adapted from the text of Treaty 1, August 3, 1871, between the Peguis
Nation and Canada.)

Cousins

I recounted as fact that virtually "every married woman and mother of a family throughout the whole extent of the Hudson's Bay territories, from the ladies of the governors of British Columbia and of the Red River Settlement downwards" was of Aboriginal descent.
– Alexander Kennedy Isbister, *Nor'Wester*, 1861

"Barney what?"

"Gargles."

"That's the name of the restaurant?"

I love Kay's laugh. It's the pitch of a crow's softer call, somewhere between a swooping croak and a "hah!"

"It used to be there, anyway."

A week after my trip to Selkirk in the cold, lunch is arranged, and my sister, Allison, and I drive up to Kay's apartment block in the south end of Winnipeg. Before the Jeep has come to a full stop, Kay is beetling out the front door, her walker ahead of her, wool hat shoved down to her eyes.

"It's not Barney's now," she says as I help her with the seat belt. "Joan called. We're going to Roxi's. Manitoba Avenue."

I want to ask her what Barney gargled but I don't.

"Joan will be there. My cousin. Yours, too, I guess."

"Here." She pokes a folded sheet of paper at me – notes about the family tree. I don't tell her she's given me the same information before. She's keen to know what I'm finding, and I'm touched by her interest. Kay is my bedrock.

"You have to write this book before I die," she says, and laughs again.

An hour or so later, after a quick drive around the town of Selkirk – I'm feeling a bit more oriented – we have made our way to the restaurant. It's lunchtime, or, in prairie-speak, "dinner," the main meal of the day. The place is crowded. At the back table, not one but three elderly people look up and wave.

"You got a birthday coming up, Kay." Kay's cousin Joan sits down beside her. Beside Joan is Eleanore. Another Eleanore? Kay's mother, daughter and cousin, all Eleanores. Three or four Catherines, two Antoines, two Kittys and three Eleanores. No wonder it's hard to keep track.

"A hundred. I never thought I'd make it."

"We're going to come into the city for it. The three of us."

Edgar, another of Kay's cousins, is beside me, wearing a crisp checked shirt. He has the distinctive white hair and intense dark eyes of my father's side of the family.

The menus open quickly. Allison and I grin at each other. My sister and brother and I have shared stories about dinners with Kay. About five-foot-six, she is slender, handsome and energetic. A few years ago, in a restaurant in St. Vital, Allison and I picked at our garden salads as Kay bent over the chicken dinner special with a side salad and fries, dinner roll, a glass of wine and a large helping of pie and ice cream.

"Well, that was good," she said, and sat back.

It must run in the family. As I sit watching the cousins – Joan, Edgar, Kay and Eleanore – tucking into their plates of sandwiches with fries and today's roast beef special, I realize how grateful I am they're alive. They're all Catherine's grandchildren, and they all have children themselves, some of whom live in Selkirk. We do have relatives here.

Why did I wait so long to explore this side of the family? My focus on my parents' divorce, especially my father's late-life antics, may have prevented me from focusing on family history. But my father's sister is my godmother, something that meant something in the days when more people were churchgoers, and her devotion to his family has been constant. When our mother and father died within four days of each other, she announced, "Well, I'm your mother now."

I look around, wondering how many others in the room are distantly related to Allison and me, or to one another.

A leaf on the family tree? Perhaps not. Some biologists challenge the metaphor of the bifurcating genealogical tree. Reproduction isn't as tidy as this – with discoveries about lateral gene transfer, we know it is possible to pick up genetic material from places other than our parents. The better metaphor might be a trellis. Trellises aren't neatly hierarchical; they wander, often create random offshoots, interact with variable environmental influences that change genetic makeup. And our genes aren't doled out evenly, either. I could share genes with both a first cousin and the woman here in the kitchen pulling a basket out of the fryer.

Grey hair, black hair, sparse hair, red hair. Small, medium, large. Around the room, I spot customers I'd characterize – if I were pressed to – as having Native roots. That's a dangerous assumption to make, and it leads to stereotyping, I know. There is so much more to cultural identity that is not and can never be about physical appearance or blood quantum. But this town near the bottom of Lake Winnipeg is, to some historians, the cradle of the Canadian West. A population of Cree, Ojibwe, Saulteaux and other migrating tribes, an influx of white settlers from Scotland, Ireland, England, Quebec, France and Iceland – all combined to create thousands of trellises of connection across the region. In that respect, Lord Selkirk's efforts to populate the West may not have failed after all.

"He was the town's mayor. Her son."

Edgar is talking to me.

I look across the table. Eleanore's eyes are abashed. She hasn't said a word during lunch, and I suspect she's shy. She's a sprite, not even ninety pounds, I'd guess, with red hair and a watchful demeanour.

"Her son." He looks at Eleanore. "He died last year."

"Your son was the mayor? I'm sorry, Eleanore." It's all I can think to say. She nods.

"Ask Edgar about the family," Kay says to me. I've noticed Kay doesn't dwell on sadness. "He's the one who knows."

As Kay and Joan and Eleanore turn to each other, Edgar starts in. I ask him what he remembers about his grandparents, Catherine Kennedy and her Quebecois husband, Antoine Couture, and as he begins to talk, I raise my eyebrows and gesture to Allison, who takes over my notebook and pen. I can't keep up with all he's telling me.

"Catherine and Antoine Couture were married in the stone church," he says.

"But Catherine was Anglican," I say. "Her parents – both Antoine Kennedy and Sally Erasmus – were baptized in the Indian church. The Church of England."

"I don't know if she turned Catholic when she married him," says Edgar. "Probably. I do know Antoine Couture wasn't going to go all the way to Winnipeg in a Red River cart to get hitched in a Roman Catholic church. It would have taken them two days."

This reaching to touch the past. As a child, I thought of Red River carts as being so distant in time. The 1870s, only two to three lifetimes ago.

"And it was George Kennedy who married them. Her uncle or brother. He was an Indian too."

Now I'm really confused. George's name hasn't come up at all so far. Of Antoine and Sally Kennedy's children, I can only find records for Catherine, John and Ann, but none named George.

I do know Catholic and Protestant religious divisions were especially strong in those days. When my grandmother married my American grandfather, Charles, in Selkirk in 1911, the Catholic Church levied a fee of $25 and exacted a vow from Charles that any "issue" from the marriage be raised Catholic. Eleanore would have it no other way.

Edgar is on a roll. "Antoine Couture and his brothers, Phillip and Louis, they came from Quebec. They all went up to the gold rush." Edgar pronounces it "kwee-beck."

"And my uncle Alfred, too?"

"Dad told me that, yes. And then Antoine came back." I don't mention the old newspaper article I found about Antoine, arrested in St. Boniface with a bag of cash and a gun. That would throw off the conversation.

"Alfred was with the North West Mounted Police out west, you know."

This, too, I'd heard before, but I can find no evidence of it. Much later, I will hear from my cousin Raymond that he inherited Alfred's NWMP gear and donated it to the RCMP headquarters in Regina.

Memory is a cracked bowl, and it fills as it empties. I wrote that once, trying to sort out my own elusive recollections. Stories handed down change, even when we think they're true. Memory researchers claim we all want to make sense, so that even credible crime witnesses fill in details to create a kind of coherence. How did the knife suddenly get from the kitchen to the dining room? Why, the intruder must have carried it.

Add to that the fact that second-hand tales become a distant relative of their original. We have busy, detail-rich minds, some of which are aging and are decades away from those conversations around the kitchen table with our families. The crumbling truths we cling to take many shapes, like third cousins once removed.

The trickster is everywhere, regardless of culture. Raven, Lugh, Coyote, Hermes –

"The men went up north by boat, stayed a few years and then came back to Manitoba. Louis became an Indian agent."

"No gold though, huh?" I ask, but that's not what I'm thinking about.

I'm looking at my cousins, knowing they're among dozens of Catherine's grandchildren who have raised dozens of children themselves. Eighty percent of Indigenous people in this country live in Western Canada and Ontario, according to Statistics Canada. Some claim one in four people in Western Canada is of Native descent, however tenuous. There is no way to quantify this, and no way without several years and a team of researchers for any of us to map out all our relations, their forebears and their descendants, regardless of their identities. Yet it gives me pause – I imagine Catherine and Antoine as a nexus, casting a wide net of relations across the globe.

And now the elderly cousins are standing together behind the table for a photo: Eleanore, Joan, Kay and Edgar. A fine-looking bunch. Kay has worn her toque all through lunch, I realize.

My heart is full. Within a year, cousins none of us know – Coutures from Alberta and Seattle, Washington – will have contacted me. Within two years, I'll have been introduced to relations in Norway House who tell me of cousins in Prince Albert and beyond.

For now, though, I'm realizing how little I know not only about Red River history but about my own. Or how they are connected.

"See you in April," Edgar says as we gather our coats.

"I can't believe I'll be a hundred," says Kay.

You Look Like an Indian

"The nurse asked me if I'd been fooling around!" my mother would say.

My sister had exotic dark hair and eyes, a warm tan complexion distinctly unlike my chalky pale skin. My mother could laugh about it all, of course, secure in her own Scottish and Irish background. We were working class for most of my childhood, and like families around us, we had no extra money, but a line was still drawn. Natives were other people.

In the schools we attended across the Prairies, my siblings and I had classmates who may have been Plains or Woodland Cree, Blackfoot, Ojibwe, Dakota, Sarcee, Swampy, Assiniboine or Métis. Perhaps even Dene who'd moved south.

We also had classmates who were Ukrainian, Icelandic, Scottish, Dutch, English, Chinese, Japanese, Irish, African-Canadian and Polish. The Western Canada in which we were raised was a mélange of First Nations people and immigrants, new or generations old.

A rolling sea of settlers, immigrants, pioneers making their way across the country. Canada is the site of over five hundred years of relationships between colonizers and the colonized. When we throw in language, religion, class, greed and power – all the noble and base faces of humanity – what we think will be a melting pot of cultures and ethnicities turns out instead to be an emulsion, a fragile mixture easy to separate under pressure or heat. From what I can tell, no distinction has been more fraught with consequences in Canada than who is white and who is not.

In Canada, two centuries of colonialist regulation of identity have parsed distinctions among Indigenous, European/British and country-born, Native-English, French Métis, Bois-Brulé, mixed blood and half-breed, among other categories. Language, policy, treaties, acts and laws have distorted – and limited – personal and complex stories of identity.

Settlers brought more than pianos, silk, rum, hymn books and diseases: they brought deeply entrenched systems of ethnocentric hierarchy and regulation to displace and destroy a way of life.

Pure laine. De souche. Old Stock. Remember those terms? The human impulse to name and to categorize, particularly where nations and ethnic groups on this soil are concerned, has changed the course of Canada.

And what is it about categories? My scholarly nerd-brain goes to the ideas of Iain McGilchrist, a psychiatrist and writer whose book, *The Master and his Emissary,* offers some insights.

Our old brain – our primal, sensory and affective side – McGilchrist claims, is the true master, but it can easily be overtaken by the so-called rational, hierarchy-loving, control-hungry, language-using region. This region is the master's emissary, meant to do the master's work. Yet McGilchrist claims human history has been distorted – to its detriment – by allowing the emissary to take over.

And so, where two or more are gathered, we must make comparisons.

We must make one an Other.

We must harden the categories.

Only three generations ago, anthropologists were measuring the human cranium to make claims about racial differences in intelligence. Around the time my great-grandmother Catherine Kennedy Couture was alive, geneticists were devoted to creating typologies to classify the range of *Homo sapiens* on the planet. Science was in love with classification, and Galileo's creed – "measure what is measurable and make measurable what is not so" – held sway. Race was an idea no one challenged. After all, it was a handy – and often visible – means of categorizing and creating hierarchies – moral, religious and social, as well as cultural.

Or: You're an Indian. And I am not.

Alexander Peter Reid, the first Dean of Medicine at Dalhousie University, jumped on the classification bandwagon in the 1870s. As a stirpiculturist – from the root *stirps*, Latin for *family origin, stock* or *stem* – he compiled a "mixed race" hierarchy, listing Red River races from "most desirable to least desirable":

1. Anglo-Saxon father and Indian mother;
2. French or French-Canadian father and Indian mother;
3. Anglo-Saxon father and mixed Anglo-Saxon and Indian mother;
4. French father and mixed French and Indian mother;
5. "Half-breed" Anglo-Saxon and Indian as father and mother;
6. "Half-breed" French and Indian as father and mother;
7. Descendants proceeding from intermarriage of the fifth class;
8 Descendants proceeding from intermarriage of the sixth class;
9. Mixed or "half-breed" father and Indian mother.

Therefore, in the Miscegenation Olympics, my ancestors would place in many of the nine categories. There are no medals, however.

What is it about race we can't get past?

A quick tour of current work in genetics helps to support what many already suspect. Noah Rosenberg and his Stanford colleagues claim up to ninety-five percent of possible genetic variation exists in any major population group. In other words, if I were to invite a few hundred people to join me at The Forks in Winnipeg – or a school in Cambridge Bay, or a stadium in Dublin or Athens, or the waterfront in Halifax – I can be certain that most of the possible genetic differences in the world would be represented. Very little genetic difference can be explained by race alone.

Then: I'm an Indian. And so are you. You're Caucasian. Or Asian. And so am I.

But hang on – as author Chelsea Vowel (âpihtawikosisân) writes: "Please stop viewing Indigenous peoples as 'the other,' but do not replace that with 'we are all Indigenous.'" Claiming we are all one can be a way to dodge responsibility for the impact of colonialism.

And how would we know anyway? Despite what ancestral records show, despite friends' and others' observations, skin colour, hair texture, shape of lips and nose are not reliable markers of ancestry. Yet even my Rock Cree friend, James, now deceased, insisted my high cheekbones and grey-white hair were markers of my ancestry.

We love our categories and our stereotypes. Biomedical ethicist Mildred Cho asks, "Why is it that we keep looking at genes and variations and organizing them into categories?" One reason, some claim, is that scientists in the fields of epidemiology and human geography can make important use of information about global and regional genetic variations.

But that's not the driving reason, as we know. The last five hundred years of migration and settlement in the "New" World have demonstrated clearly – and to great devastation – there are social and political advantages to defining and mapping race.

Geneticists today are rarely among the wealthy and powerful whose investment in maintaining cultural difference benefits and furthers a cause. True, it was as late as 1906 when the Kellogg patriarch co-founded the Race Betterment Foundation, and as late as 1903 when the American Breeders' Association was founded (with Alexander Graham Bell as one of its members). What is and is not purebred has always had an appeal. Yet scientific racism seems to be on the wane, even as structural (including governmental and institutional) racism persists.

The bottom line: even if culture and society paid attention to current genetics research and resisted categorizing us all into race divisions and gradations, those who identify as Indigenous in Canada continue to be forced to live as "Indian" in colonial Canada.

In other words, where distinctions of race are concerned, there is still only power.

A Nail in Old Wood

Months later, spring is on its way and I've returned to Manitoba, along with dozens of Kay's relatives, to celebrate her hundredth birthday. Cake, homemade wine, dozens of her friends and family. Flowers, gifts and countless birthday cards, one of which is signed by Canada's twenty-second prime minister. Most everyone except Kay rolls their eyes at the sight of it.

And my aunt, sharp as usual, is smartly dressed in a wine-coloured suit, laughing and posing as everyone lines up for photos and more photos.

The next day, my eldest brother, Brian, decides to drive up to Selkirk with me. It's May first and the snow is gone. After more research, I'm clearer about which church is which. Through social media, I've tracked down and contacted Wendy, the caretaker of St. Peter, Dynevor church, and have made plans to meet her there.

When we arrive in Selkirk, Brian waits in the car while I choose a bouquet of flowers and, just to be on the safe side, ask the clerk about the best route to the stone church.

"Stone church?"

The human telegraph starts up.

The clerk calls over to the man in produce, who calls over to the guy stocking a shelf, who is now walking down to ask the cashier at the checkout on the end. Mouths move and the message makes its way back across the store.

"Across the river. You go north and then over the bridge, or south to Lockport and north from there. You can follow the river road if you...." I can feel my eyes glaze over, but I recover, still wondering how many know about this historic landmark.

Well, I'm not one to judge. I didn't know.

"So?" Brian says. I hand him the flowers and put the car into gear.

"I think I've got this."

WENDY IS DEVOTED TO THIS LAND, this church. Outside, the spring rain is gentle. When we park, she emerges from her house, a few hundred yards from the church building. Her pleasant face and matter-of-fact manner immediately draw me in.

As the three of us make our way around the church, Wendy shows us the remains of the spire, recently decimated by woodpeckers; the original altar and wood floor; two wood stoves, their chimneys high in the rafters. When the church was built, only one stove heated the building. Nowadays, the church is used mostly in winter; its companion on the other side of the river, the white wood church, is used year-round.

I finally understand. Both are St. Peter's church and both – along with a smaller church long gone – have been known at some point as the Indian church.

In a room left of the altar, Wendy points out artifacts her ancestors have cared for. She knows every inch of this building – three generations of her family have tended it; her eyes are lit with pride as she walks us from one spot to the next.

Open-air cracks are around the edges of the gothic window at the front.

"Come back and see the stained glass when it's finished," she says. I wonder how repairs are paid for, but I don't ask. The Peguis Nation, perhaps? The Manitoba government?

From inside, gothic windows around both sides of the church give the space a gently charged atmosphere, and the quiet makes me feel porous, open to the land and the river, as though the church is merely the palm of a hand in which we're held.

Brian and I pause in the aisle to run our fingers along hand-hewn pews that have survived their makers by a century and a half.

I return to the nave area, where a couple would have stood to take each other's hands in marriage. Antoine Kennedy and Sally (Sarah) Erasmus, Catherine's parents, were married in the Indian church on December 23, 1847. A Thursday, the day most marriages were held in Rupert's Land back then. But it can't have been this church, this building.

Outside, the rain is falling steadily. Brian and I walk among the graves – large stone monuments, flat stone markers, slim white wooden crosses. Peguis's gravestone is here, among those of others in the Peguis Nation. We are looking for Kennedy, Erasmus or Budd, and we're having no luck.

I am reminded of Louise Bernice Halfe's words: "Years ago, I visited the graveyard on the reserve / and counted all the dead." Her work describes great losses her ancestors suffered.

Yet finding the names is a challenge.

"There were fires," says Wendy. "A lot of the crosses were burned. So many were buried here, but now their names are gone."

Fire, disaster, separation, epidemics – so much loss, and yet ancestors from many directions who kept on keeping on. I smile as a quirky image comes to mind. Each of us – or the idea of us – whooshing through the centuries and roaring out the end of the cosmic pipe, into the stark cold of the present. Shocked, alert. So near our ancestors and yet so far.

After walking through rows of graves, we reach a bench and, beside it, a pile of decaying beams Wendy rescued from church renovations years ago.

She holds up a piece of wood. "When I think about it," she says, "those beams lasted 160 years, and as trees they were already over a hundred years old. See the nails they used back then?"

Following the River

Catherine Kennedy wasn't born when this wood was brought up-river. But her parents, Sally and Antoine, were here, and perhaps their remains still are. Later, I will learn Antoine Kennedy worked as a carpenter in the community, but now it's all mist and cloud to me. I place my fingers on the pile of old, rotting beams and want to reach through to the hands that laid them for the foundation.

At the bus stop, Brian and I wait for his ride back to Winnipeg. When we left Wendy at the church, I tried to drive back to the other side of town to show him the cemetery where Catherine was buried, but I became turned around again.

"I'm usually not this clueless."

"Don't worry about it," my brother says. "I'll be back."

I resolve the next day to match sites with some of the stories about the Selkirk area, and to return once more to the stone church and those crumbling beams. I plan to meet a man at the library who has been researching the history of Selkirk steamships, and to visit Edgar, the cousin Kay calls their historian. During my lunch with Kay, Allison and our elderly cousins, Edgar had offered to answer any questions I had.

As I watch the bus head south carrying my Ottawa-bound brother, the sun comes out and, drawing on the stubbornness I was born with, I take one more tour around Selkirk to find the cemetery, hoping by this time of year, the gates are open.

They are. The ground is wet and muddy, but I can walk among the graves, take a few photos and read the names on Catherine's burnt-bronze tombstone. Catherine Couture's name is at the top, but the other names are not familiar. More research ahead. Perhaps Edgar will know.

When I return to Winnipeg, I browse a book about Chief Peguis and am startled to find a list of the first communicants in the stone church: 127 souls.

And there they are: *Antoin Kennedy and his wife, Salle.*

November 19, 1854. Brian and I had walked where they walked, stood where they stood, touched the same pews. Two years later, Allison and I will visit the church on a sunny day – the glow from the new stained glass window is like coloured scarves on the old wood.

BACK IN NOVA SCOTIA, I am careful as I unpack my bag. Inside a paper box from the hotel toiletries, I have wrapped in tissue what I found on the ground under the pile of crumbling wood behind the church: a half-inch flat-headed nail, typical of the crudely wrought hardware of the past. A nail among thousands hammered as the church took shape over 160 years ago. In the mulch of decaying wood, it was on its way back to earth. I'd looked around for Wendy to ask her if she'd mind if I brought it home with me, but she'd returned to the house.

Before I returned to the car, I reached in my backpack for one of the stones I'd brought from the Atlantic coast and laid it on the ground.

Two landscapes, two home places: a conversation between the shores of the river and the shores of the sea. Later, I emailed Wendy to tell her I'd return the nail.

"Keep it," she wrote back. "It was meant to be."

"A Nail in Old Wood." Image of St. Peter Dynevor Stone Church.
Photo by author

Mere Etymology

HALFBREED.

The word "Halfbreed" is heard or used here every day in the year. There is such a large number of those popularly designated as "Halfbreeds"—a vast majority of the people of Red River, in fact—and they are so interwoven in all movements and concerns of the place, that they must, of necessity, be constantly mentioned. A European takes to himself, as wife, one of the native Indian women, and his offspring we call Halfbreeds. An Indian marries a European or, at least, a white woman, and his progeny bear the same appellation. And the reason usually assigned is that said offspring or progeny are literally half-breeds,—half white, half red—or, if you will, half one race, half another, half Caucasian half Indian. Were this the extent of the application of the name, the explanation would be passable; but the name is given equally to those who may have a White father and Halfbreed mother, or vice versa, and who are, thus, quarter-breeds—if we accept the reason of the name Half breed above given as sound. In this country in fact, the name applies to all who have Indian blood in a greater or less degree. This is the general acceptation of the term, and, in this sense nine-tenths or more of the civilised people of Rupert's Land are "Halfbreeds."

"Halfbreed" from Nor'Wester, 1862.

Stranger Things

A thicket of mysteries. Earlier in the year, I sat at my desk in Nova Scotia, trying to make the image on the screen larger. So far, I can find only one photograph of Catherine, a snapshot of her standing with my grandmother, Eleanore, in front of the house in Selkirk. It's blurry.

But I now have one I've copied from Kay – a formal portrait of Antoine and Catherine Couture and all their children – and it doesn't look right no matter how much I zoom in.

Something about the exposure? Damage to the print?

In the late nineteenth century, camera exposure times were much longer than most smiles, which, aside from social mores, may account for so many serious faces. And exposure times made it difficult for parents – usually the mother – to keep the young and squirmy from moving about.

The solution must have seemed logical at the time. Simply drape cloth, patterned curtains, a cloak – anything – over the mother to disguise her as flowered furniture, sit the child on her lap and pretend the photograph doesn't look like little Maisy is resting in the arms of an earlier version of Darth Vader. Ghoulish and comical, these images became common.

But as far as I know, no one is hidden behind shrouds in this family portrait of Catherine, Antoine and their children. I am hoping cousin Edgar will help.

I drive around Selkirk and pass the rusting hulk of the old steam-boat, a curiosity in the reedy waters behind Taylor Avenue. Edgar will know about this, too.

We sit at the kitchen table in his tidy bungalow and I pepper him with questions. Whose names are those on Catherine's tombstone in the St. Michael's cemetery?

"The gravestone is wrong," he says. "Catherine's birthdate is wrong. Antoine's birthdate is wrong, too. He was born in 1847. It took a long time before the fish company came up with the money."

The Dominion Fish Company, owner of the SS *Premier*. Did this mean they accepted responsibility for the disaster?

"Someone used the wrong records." Edgar's voice is quiet. His eyes look lost in thought.

"And those other names? Phillip, Lucille, Roy and Lorna?"

"Phillip was their youngest – he died of epilepsy. And the others were their grandchildren."

Thank heavens for Edgar, family historian. What he tells me doesn't jibe with the stapled sheet of family history my father spent years gathering, the result of many road trips and visits to government offices. My father wanted most of all to affirm his American roots on his father's side, hoping for dual Canadian-American citizenship. On the typed sheets are incomplete dates and names, some for his mother Eleanore's roots. He mentions Catherine's death and Warren's Landing. No mention of her ancestry.

Edgar leads me downstairs to the rec room to look at photographs.

"By the way, the old ship in the slough at the end of Eveline Street – is there a story to that?"

"Oh, that. Some dentist bought it after it was decommissioned and wanted to use it for floating entertainment – parties, music and the like. He couldn't get a license."

When I reach the bottom of the stairs and look toward the back of the panelled room, I spot it. The original photograph, large-scale.

Edgar lists them all for me, left to right: George, Catie, Napoleon, Eleanore, Theodore, Mabel, Alfred, Nettie, Malvena, Edgar and Phillip.

And sitting in the middle is Antoine, their father. Beside him, a strange-looking creature. The one whose head looked wonky in my tiny copy of the photograph. The head is lopsided, doesn't conform to the shape and gesture of the shoulders and neck it rests on.

"Edgar, this is weird."

"It was taken after she was dead, you know."

Who does that?

It was common in the Victorian era to prop up dead bodies for photographs – the image might be the only chance for the bereaved to have a picture of their beloved. But that wouldn't have been true in this case.

"Stranger Things." Couture family. Image courtesy of Katherine (Kay) Reynaud and Edgar Couture.

"They had someone sit in. And the photographer took an old pho-tograph, cut it to fit."

Of course. It's from the only photograph I've found so far – the one of Eleanore and Catherine outside their house on Taylor Avenue.

Headstones, disembodied heads, rusting hulks. Curiouser and curiouser.

Some of Catherine's children would have moved away from Selkirk by the time Catherine died. Catie had been living near Seattle, but she may have returned to work up in Warren's Landing with her father. Did they use the occasion of Catherine's funeral to take the family portrait? Would they all have received a copy of this as a keepsake?

And there's Eleanore, in the middle behind Catherine. What must it have been like to stand behind someone else's body wearing your mother's clothes, holding still until the exposure was complete, feel-ing such profound absence?

Part Two: Her Many Names

Indian woman
faded black & white
whispers of a long gone past
like horses and fur trading.
– Rosanna Deerchild, "We are Just"

Ordinary Odyssey – Her Many Names –
A Lineage of Foremothers: 1758 to 1908

Ordinary Odyssey

Men go on journeys:

14 Friday. We travelled 6 miles S.W.b.S. Country hilly, producing short Grass, low willows & ponds in places; also many vermin holes: our Course very uncertain; I found it inconvenient to use the Compass: Indian Leaders, whom the Natives say are intending to go to war, are many; but we expect to see some of them before the season for these expeditions; when I hope to prevail on them to desist. The Friends of the Child who died Yesterday, make great lamentation, pricking themselves with Arrows in the Arms, sides, thighs and legs & the women scratching their legs &c with flints.

22 Tuesday. This day the Natives pitched a very large tent. The men singing, &c, & the Women dancing; & all dressed in their most gaudy apparel: A cold collation of berries dressed up with fat.

23 Wednesday. Indians employed: Men conjuring, & Women dancing; All this is done for the recovery of the sick.

Matthew Cocking – transcriber, journal-keeper, recorder – arrives in York Factory in 1765 to work for the Hudson's Bay Company. My five – or is it six? – times great-grandfather.

In travels inland to promote the company, he keeps a journal. Cocking refers to women in his notes more frequently than most colonials of his generation. But, like them, he has alliances with many women – three on record – and sires three daughters. One of his country wives is an Ininiwiskwêw from Severn House, southeast of York Factory. He and Ke-che-cho-wick (Kahnapawanakan) dance their way to the birth of their daughter, Wash-e-soo-E'Squew.

And so begins a story, like many other stories.

Ke-che-cho-wick (Kahnapawanakan), the woman from Severn, is a part of the Homeguard Cree (Maskêkowininiwak) community, people at HBC posts who supply the company with game meat, provisions and information to promote the fur trade, travel and survival. The men are tripmen, seasonal labourers and hunters; the women are companions and sleeping dictionaries, all necessary to the success of the trade.

Matthew Cocking and Ke-che-cho-wick's daughter, Wash-e-soo-E'Squew, is born, it seems, when he became master at Severn House. Her name (*wa-shisoo* means she is bright, she shines) suggests her birthplace. The *sh* sound was, apparently, found only along the coast of Hudson Bay. A couple of years after his daughter is born, Cocking returns to York, England, and dies at fifty-six, leaving a small amount of financial support for Wash-e-soo-E'Squew.

Women, too, go on journeys:

Wash-e-soo-E'Squew travels to York Factory for years to collect the allowance her father has willed her. When she sees the beginnings of a company school, she recognizes its benefits. Her spouse, Muskego Budd, dies, and when Wash-e-soo-E'squew becomes destitute, she travels farther south to Norway House with her children.

In Norway House, Reverend John West takes an interest in Wash-e-soo-E'Squew's bright young son, Sakachuweskum, and offers to take the boy down to the fledgling Red River settlement for an education. This is unusual: the HBC doesn't exactly encourage the Church

Missionary Society to take Indigenous children away from the forts – they're too useful as workers.

Nevertheless, Wash-e-soo-E'Squew takes up Reverend West's offer, and two years later, in 1822, she joins her son in Red River. By this time, Sakachuweskum is known by his Christian name, Henry Budd. In 1828, William Cockran baptizes Henry's mother, too, and Wash-e-soo-E'Squew's name becomes Mary (Cocking) Budd. Knowing the value of reading and writing and Christianity, Mary Budd sends her other children to school in Red River as well.

Henry grows up to be a missionary in Rupert's Land. Catherine (Kitty), another of Mary's six children, is born in 1805 in Norway House. As a young woman, she meets HBC worker Peter Erasmus, and they, too, join the family migration to Red River, where they are church wed by William Cockran.

Now we are in the Red River settlement, which, by the 1830s, is doubling in population. The 1821 merger of HBC and NWC had resulted in job losses for Native workers, who were encouraged to settle in Red River. Kitty and Peter raise seven children, one of whom, Peter Erasmus Jr., becomes an explorer and translator out west.

Another of the Erasmus children, Sally (Sarah), stays in Red River and marries a member of Chief Henry Prince's band. Antoine Kennedy is close to twenty years Sally's senior, and they, too, have several children.

One of those, born in late December 1858, is Catherine Kennedy.

Catherine Kennedy is an ordinary woman who, at the age of forty-nine, boards a steamer to travel from Selkirk to Norway House, the territory of her grandmothers.

Journeys into archives; two-hundred-year-old texts; frayed and crumbling church registers; scrip records; lost leads; diaries; graveyards; artifacts; conversations with relatives, Indigenous observers and scholars – and I find traces. She was alive. Her paths gave her granddaughters life, left us faint tracks we try to follow.

Seven lifetimes back to Ke-che-cho-wick in the eighteenth century,
then forward
  to Wash-e-soo-E'Squew (Mary Cocking Budd),
    and to Kitty Erasmus, then
      Sally Kennedy, then to

Catherine Kennedy Couture,
my great-grandmother, and her passage in 1908 to the top of Lake
Winnipeg.

And we come to another beginning.

From the confluence of different faiths and tongues and forces;
from pro-Indigenous, pro-Métis and pro-Canadian; from Swampy
Cree (Ininiwak/Maskêkowininiwak) lying down with Danes (who
might have been Swedes), Englishmen, Americans, Scots, Irishmen
and Quebecois. People who speak Cree, English, Bungi, Gaelic and
French. Nurturers and murderers, comforters and nursemaids, translators and tripmen, explorers, thieves and Indian agents, bison hunters,
pemmican makers, ministers, cooks, rounders and wanderers, teach-
ers, fishers and farmers.

Each of us contains multitudes, as the poet Whitman says. Each
of us walks with stories coursing, roaring downstream. We all travel
inside the past: everything that once was still is. Our histories are frag-
mented, incomplete, contestable; they brought us here, and they carry
us forward.

Her Many Names

frost exploding
the great moon
eagle
goose
frog
egg laying
feather moulting
flying up
rutting
migrating
freeze up
hoarfrost
long nights she waxes and wanes, is new, crescent, quarter,
gibbous, full. To some, a mirror of emotion, to others,
Queen of Life and Death. Hecate,
       Grandmother, Luna, Eternal One.
Works tides, holds a lantern to the dark, promises renewal
and perseverance. Without her, we are not. Learn
under her watch: strength, courage, respect, how
to scrabble for truth, be guided by
honesty, walk with humility.

Grandmothers Ke-che-cho-wick, Wash-e-soo-E'Squew,
Kitty (Catherine), Sally and Catherine –

under the same moons as cousins, strangers,
the unnamed, notorious, ordinary, extraordinary,
your stations in life
       both promise and threat;
The Bible, solace
            and weapon; blood, the source
of strength and shame. Few of you knew old age. I sift
for detail in the words of those who whittle lives with a pen,
a rare instrument for a woman. A shred, debris, a tendril –
a past you lived we cannot fully know. Not the rustle
of your coats, footsteps in the night air, the touch of silken
or calloused hands. The tangy scent of ashes cooled
in the hearth. Wisdom –
       in the stirring of life under sugar moon,
storms of thunder moon, in falling-leaves moon when
loss is all around. You have watched the river rise
and fall, known it packed with ice, muddy
in spring rain, swift in summer. A red stream.
Many granddaughters later, countless first cries
and graves, and here I am, time waning.
The moon glints on the river,
water rises like blood.

A Lineage of Foremothers:
1758 to 1908

Who is lied about, who is suppressed
who is showcased and honoured and no, wait, listen –
who is allowed a natural life.
– Joanne Arnott, "Truth & Wreck"

Begin in the days of **Ke-che-cho-wick** (w/Matthew Cocking)
b. circa 1758 (also known as Kahnapawanakan)
5x Great-Grandmother
             then to the days of her daughter
Wash-e-soo-E'Squew Cocking (w/Muskego Budd)
b. 1780 (baptized Mary Budd in Red River)
4x Great-Grandmother
             and to those of Mary's daughter
Catherine/Kitty Budd (w/Peter Erasmus Sr.)
b. 1805
3x Great-Grandmother
             and those of Kitty's daughter
Sarah/Sally Erasmus (w/Antoine Kennedy) b. 1830
Great-Great-Grandmother
             and finally to the days of Sally's daughter
Catherine Kennedy Couture (w/Antoine Couture)
b. 1858
Great-Grandmother

Ke–che–cho–wick (Kahnapawanakan)

Ke-che-cho-wick (Kahnapawanakan) –
Wanted: Fur Trade Wife – Pimîhkân Maker –
Woman with an Axe

Ke–che–cho–wick
(Kahnapawanakan)

b. circa 1758 – date of death unconfirmed

Woman of Severn
born along the river
a few hundred miles southeast
of York Factory at the edge
of Hudson Bay –
near Severn House, the meeting place
for Company trade tucked under
Partridge Island on a map.

One of the Homeguard Cree,
the second of Cocking's women,
mother of Wash-e-soo-E'Squew,
a name on a page as far back
as I can reach.

Wanted: Fur Trade Wife

She was his for a bottle of
plonk or a bundle of tobacco, but
it would be pretty swell if you
got one or even two horses.
– Garry Thomas Morse, "Squaw"

1. Rest with him.
2. Make *bouilli* – boil pieces of fresh meat with potatoes and, if available, salt, savory and sage.
   (Where there is no metal pot, drop hot stones into vessels made of skins.)
3. Pitch a tipi (with other women – men aren't as efficient).
4. Pick berries, gather spruce roots for the seams of canoes and harvest birch bark.
5. Dry meat by the fire or on a summer day. Pound to a powder. Add bison fat and, if available, berries. Stuff into bison skins. Prepare enough for long trips.
6. Rest with him.
7. Weave sinew for snowshoes.
8. Sew moccasins and other clothing, including your own leggings.
9. Bear his child.
10. Carry packs in travel. Must be highly skilled in the art of compact stowing, folding, using every square inch.

Pimîhkân Maker

Fat and moose meat. Fat and beaver. Fat and elk. Fat from bone marrow is the best. (Don't waste the fat on candles.) Pound the meat to dust. Haul it out to the trough, melt the tallow from the animals, pour it in the trough and mix. Some say fifty pounds of meat, forty of grease is a good ratio. Add chokecherries, saskatoons, wild pears and blueberries, if you can, especially if there's a wedding in the offing. Wait until the mixture is cold. Sew it up in large bags of buffalo parchment, hair still on. It will keep for a year or more and travel well. A handful is a meal and fills the belly in the cold, on the water, in the bush. When settlers come, they'll want to mix it up a bit. Make rubaboo by boiling the pemmican with onions and potatoes; maybe throw in a wild turnip or two. Or make rowshow: shred the pemmican, add flour and water. If you're with an Orkney man, add oatmeal. Fry it up. Try to use the best parts of the buffalo, the tongues and the bosses. They are the most delicate.

Woman with an Axe

Being a story set eleven kilometres from York Factory at Notawatowi Sipi, "the creek from which you fetch the people," recorded by the explorer and map-maker known as Koo-koo-sint or "the stargazer," and featuring Bruin, Wm. Budge, John Mellam and the Woman with an Axe.

The smell of grouse cooking attracted a Polar Bear, who marched to the Tent, and around it, his heavy tread was heard, and no more cooking thought of. As usual in the evening, the fowling pieces were being washed and cleaned, and were then not lit for use, but there was a loaded Musquet. At length Bruin found the door, and thrust in his head and neck, the Tent Poles prevented further entrance. Budge climbed up the tent poles and left Mellam and his Indian woman to fight the Bear, the former snatched up the Musquet, it snapped; seizing it by the muzzle he broke off the stock on the head of the Bear, and then with hearty blows applied the barrel and lock to his head; the Indian woman caught up her axe on the other side of the door, and in like manner struck Bruin on the head, such an incessant storm of blows [as] made him withdraw himself; he went to the Hoard and began to tear it in pieces, for the game; a fowling piece was quickly dried, loaded with two balls, and fired into him, the wound was mortal, he went a few paces and fell with a dreadful growl.

Budge now wanted to descend from the smoky top of the Tent, but the Woman with her axe in her hand heaped wood on the fire and threatened to brain him if he came down. He begged hard for his life, she was determined, fortunately, Mellam snatched the axe from her, but she never forgave him, for the Indian woman pardons Man for everything but want of courage, this is her sole support and protection; there are no laws to defend her.

Wash–e–soo–E'Squew
(Mary Budd)

Wash–e–soo–E'Squew Cocking
(later, Mary Budd)

b. 1780 – d. 1850

daughter of Ke-che-cho-wick
and Matthew Cocking, born near
Severn, you travelled to the fort
for the annuity your father left:
six pounds "laid out in Ginger Bread, Nuts &tc.
as they have no other means of obtaining these little
luxuries, with which the paternal fondness of a Father
formally provided them."

Like so many
women of your day, generic,
like canned peas, no-name,
all-purpose
Aggathas.

Here W. H. Cook, a trader and your uncle by
country marriage, tries to sort out the
inheritance, claiming you, like the rest,
are no dabster at arithmetic.

Following the River

Red River, 25 May 1825

My Dear Sir:

Could I ask the favor of you to inform me the state of the Annuitants'
Accounts who are designated by the names of Agathas, Washihow Esqow
& Keshechow e cummicoot – my partner is one of these (Agathas) & her
arrears of 3 years accumulation were last Summer £10.18.10 – instead
of the net sum of £18 – some wrong payment of this annuity must have
taken place owing to the Gentm at the Factory not being able to identify
the parties –

the name of Agathas being an Appelation suitable to any of the Half-
Breed Ladies – Mr. Jones informs me that a Box7 procured by Mr. West
on behalf of Washeho Esqow was marked with the name Agathas – from
which I conclude that the Arrears of Annuity taken by Mr. West for
Washeho Esqow was debited to Agathas – & thus the deficiency in my
wife's Acct may have occurred –

Washehow Esqow on the other hand complains of the deficiency of her
account but she being a resident at Norway House & no doubt frequently
applying to the Store for supplies of Prov' etc may have overrun her reckon-
ing before she was aware of it, for like the rest she is no dabster at arith-
metic & would have no Idea of the limit to which she could proceed with
the ample or rather enormous sum of £6 annually.

Any little information you can afford on the foregoing matter will greatly
oblige.
Yours sincerely
W. H. Cook

You become the wife of Muskego Budd,
and on Budd's death, you make your way down
to Red River where the Reverend William Cockran
brings you into the Christian fold.

On May 11, 1828, you become
Mary Budd.

It's that easy.

Call Her Aggathas

Virgin martyr, third century, pious
and beautiful, Agathas is brought before
the governor of Sicily, Quintianus,
but spurns his advances. He imprisons
her in a brothel, and later, when
she continues to refuse his tongue
and cock, he ties her to a pillar
and cuts off her breasts.

As one might expect.

Thus Agathas is given immortality in
the Canon of the Mass, right up there
with the Virgin Mary herself. Aggie:
patron saint of bell-ringers.

In early days of the trade, Aggathas
was everywhere (one *g* or two, one *s*
or none) – easier perhaps than Her, She,
the Woman, Squaw from Severn, Woman
on Foot, Thing One and Thing Two, or a numbered
cast member in a crowd scene of an epic movie.
A name to make a category, not a woman.

But why Aggathas? Is the name melodic,
resonant, does it warm the sensibilities
of a man cleft from the bosom of his mother
country, scrabbling in the bush for the riches
of a new landscape and, with luck, reaping
the reward of warm brown legs wrapped
around his haunches? Aggathas,
Aggathas on his dry lips, ringing
a bell that wants ringing?

Bride

Testamentum from the diary of Daniel Williams Harmon, fur trader:

Payet one of my Interpreters, has taken one of the Natives Daughters for a Wife, and to her Parents he gave in Rum & dry Goods etc. to the value of two hundred Dollars, and all the cerimonies [sic] attending such circumstances are that when it becomes time to retire, the Husband or rather Bridegroom (for as yet they are not joined by any bonds) shews his Bride where his Bed is, and then they, of course both go to rest together, and so they continue to do as long as they can agree among themselves, but when either is displeased with their choice, he or she will seek another Partner, which is law here.

Dressed

Testamentum from the records of Alexander Mackenzie, explorer:

Their shoes are commonly plain, and their leggins gartered beneath the knee. The coat, or body covering, falls down to the middle of the leg, and is fastened over the shoulder with cords, a flap or cape turning down about eight inches, both before and behind, and agreeably ornamented with quill-work and fringe; the bottom is also fringed, and fancifully painted as high as the knee. As it is very loose, it is enclosed round the waist with a stiff belt, decorated with tassel, and fastened behind. The arms are covered to the wrists, with detached sleeves, which are sewed as far as the bend of the arm; from thence they are drawn up to the neck, and the corners of them fall down behind, as low as the waist. The cap, when they wear one, consists of a certain quantity of leather or cloth, sewed at one end, by which means it is kept on the head, and, hanging down the back, is fastened to the belt, as well as under the chin.

The upper garment is a robe like that worn by the men. Their hair is divided on the crown, and tied behind, or sometimes fastened in large knots over the ears. They are fond of European articles, and prefer them to their own Native commodities. Their ornaments consist in common with all savages, in bracelets, rings, and similar baubles. Some of the women tattoo three perpendicular lines, which are sometimes double: one from the center of the chin to that of the under lip, and one parallel on either side to the corner of the mouth.

One of the Ingrates

Testamentum on the Abyss of Heathenism by the Reverend Abraham
Cowley (1816–1877), assigned to Red River in the 1840s:

Ezekiel 37:2…and behold, there were very many in
the open valley; and, lo, they were very dry.
And He said to me, "Son of man, can these bones live?"

My soul yearns over these people
and I think I would willingly spend all my days
in trying to secure them from destruction. Sometimes,
however, it is otherwise, when I witness their callous

indifference to spiritual things, their tenacity in their own
superstitious vanities, their almost entire want of gratitude or
any good feeling, indeed, their wolf-like disposition.

I feel inclined to let them alone.

What can possibly be done with such a people?
But then I ask who made any to differ? I cannot the same
almighty power create these anew. Thus again I am constrained
to persevere,
>   *hoping even against hope*
>   *these dry bones shall live.*

A Bird in the Bush

Testamentum on half-breed women by Alexander Ross, Councillor of Assiniboia, also known as The Professor, 1783–1856:

...I invited my friend to accompany me to the upper part of the settlement, as he was anxious to know what kind of life the Canadians and half-breeds lead.

The women are invariably fairer than the men. They are not highcoloured, but pale and sallow, resembling in their complexion more the Natives of Spain, or the south of France, than the swarthy Indians here.

My companion remarked: "Your half-breed women are fairer in complexion than Canadian women, but their extreme bashfulness deprives them of the graceful address peculiar to white women."

Half-breed women are exceedingly well-featured and comely – many even handsome, and those who have the means tidy about their person and dress. They are fond of show, invariably attire themselves in gaudy prints, and shawls, chiefly of the tartan kind – all of foreign manufacture, but, like Indian women, they are very tenacious of the habits and customs of their Native country.

The blanket is used on all occasions, not only here, but throughout the continent, both at home and abroad; if a stick is wanted for the fire, or a pleasure party is to be joined away from home, the blanket is called for. This habit gives them a stooping gait, and the constant use of the same blanket, day and night, wet and dry, is supposed to give rise to consumptive complaints, which they are all subject to.

Following the River

At the age of thirty years, they look as old as a white woman of forty, perhaps from the fact that they marry young, and keep their children long at the breast. We have noticed the extreme bashfulness, their false modesty or shyness, similar to what is observable among the Formosans. Although many understand and speak both French and English, they are averse to speak any other language than their mother tongue.

And if the traveller chance to meet one of them on the road, she will instantly shroud her head in her blanket, and try to pass without speaking. Speak to her, and she looks to the ground. Stop, and she turns to one side, and ten to one passes without answering you. For one of her own countrymen, however, a smile, a "bonjour" and a shake of the hand is always ready.

Like a bird in the bush, they are always on the move. It is not uncommon for a woman getting up in the morning to throw her blanket about her and set off on a gossiping tour among her neighbours, and leave her children foodless and clothes-less among the ashes, to shift for themselves; yet, like most Indian women, they are generally tender mothers. We hope the ladies alluded to will take a useful lesson from these remarks. And likewise reform their shopping propensity and love of fineries, which do not bespeak industrious habits, or a great desire to manufacture their own clothing. These are blemishes not easily removed.

Taking them all in all, they are a happy people. The women are great tea-drinkers; but seldom indulge in the luxury of sugar with this beverage. Debts may accumulate, creditors may press, the labourer may go without his hire, the children run naked, but the tea kettle and tobacco pipe are indispensable. They are passionately fond of roving about, visiting, card-playing and making up gossiping parties.

All comers and goers are welcome guests at their board. The apostle recommends hospitality; but we cannot give the name of hospitality to the foolish and ruinous practice we are speaking of: strictly following the Indian principle "Divide while anything remains," and beg when all is done. This habit is carried to excess, as most things are, the indulgence of which reduces them to misery and want.

Far be it from us to find fault with a people for attachment to their own ancient usages; but all men must condemn a practice that not only fosters poverty in the individual homes, but is, in its consequences, injurious to society.

Catherine (Kitty)
Budd Erasmus

Catherine (Kitty) Budd Erasmus – Niwikimakan: Life with a Man –
Instructions for Turning Off – People on the Stage – Teacher –
Polka Queen – Tall Poppy: How to Write a Red River Tragedy

Catherine (Kitty) Budd Erasmus

b. 1805 – d. 1890

daughter of Mary Budd,
sister of Henry, wife of Peter Erasmus Sr.
mother of Peter Erasmus Jr., Sally
and five more –

Who are you when you're not someone else's something?

You lived through the devastation of 1846. January was influenza, May was measles, epidemics minor compared to "the bloody flux" that arrived in June. Alexander Ross wrote: "hardly anything to be seen but the dead on their way to their last home; nothing to be heard but the tolling of bells…from the 18 of June to the 2 of August, the deaths averaged seven a day, or 321 in all; being one out of every sixteen of our population…. On one occasion, thirteen burials were proceeding at once."

Many houses were emptied; no living family member remained.

Somehow, Kitty, your family made it through.

Your son, Peter, who would move farther west to work as a translator and settle in Whitefish Lake, remembers stories of home.

He recalls the Scotsman who lived next door to you in St. Andrews and worked sun-up to sundown with his ox and his hand plow. A man always grousing at the ox.

"Peter," you'd said to your husband, "see about our neighbour. He hasn't been out of the house these last two days. He may be sick as he worked all through the rain Saturday and Sunday."

"He'll not thank me," Peter had said, "and probably dress me down for my curiosity."

Later, as an old man, your son Peter recalls:

"Dad, without further words, simply rolled the old chap in his blankets and packed him over to our house. Spluttering with anger and cussing all the way availed him not at all, and with Dad's size and strength, his efforts to get away were useless. 'Be quiet, you little beggar! You are going to stay here till you are better.'"

Then your husband called for you, Kitty. You came into the room, "with some hot potion for the patient to drink as well as other remedies to apply to his chest. The old gentleman objected to the exposure of his chest, but with Dad's forcible assistance, the medicine was applied.

"Father stood waiting in the other room, and when he caught the Scot trying to dress himself, he took away his clothes, leaving only a woman's dress that happened to be in the room."

The man later recovered, as you know, and the two became fast friends, a pairing that amused and perplexed your neighbours.

Your son Peter remembers how you kept your eight children clothed and fed:

"Our clothes were leather pants with a soft deerskin coat, cotton shirts, Indian moccasins with blanket duffels for our feet. The girls wore print dresses with, I believe, homemade knitted underwear."

Your girls: Sophia, Catherine, Sally and the youngest, Mary Anne.

"The boys wore nothing else, winter or summer. The moccasins were either moosehide or buffalo skin, as they were considered warmer and more durable.

"I do not remember being really cold with these meagre clothes. Perhaps it was the strong foods we ate that helped us resist the cold.

Meat was always our main diet. Buffalo were plentiful, and few men of
that day ever thought they would be completely killed out."
   Kitty, three times great-grandmother:
   nursemaid, cook, knitter, seamstress, wife, mother.

Niwikimakan: Life with a Man

Testamentum from the journal of Reverend John West, First Protestant Minister in Rupert's Land, 1778–1845:

The blasphemy of the men, in the difficulties they had to encounter, was truly painful to me. I had hoped better things of the Scotch, from their known moral and enlightened education; but their horrid imprecations proved a degeneracy of character in Indian country.

This, I lamented to find, was too generally the case with Europeans, particularly so in their barbarous treatment of women. They do not admit them as their companions, nor do they allow them to eat at their tables, but degrade them merely as slaves to their arbitrary inclinations; while the children grow up wild and uncultivated as the heathen.

April 6. One of the principal settlers informed me this morning that an Indian had stabbed one of his wives in a fit of intoxication at an encampment near his house. I immediately went to the lodge to inquire into the circumstances, and found that the poor woman had been stabbed in wanton cruelty, through the shoulder and the arm, but not mortally. The Indians were still drunk, and some of them having knives in their hands, I thought it most prudent to withdraw from their tents, without offering any assistance. The Indians appear to me to be generally of an inoffensive and hospitable disposition; but spirituous liquors, like war, infuriate them with the most revengeful and barbarous feelings. They are so conscious of this effect of drinking that they generally deliver up

*their guns, bows and arrows, and knives to the officers before they begin
to drink at the Company's Post; and when at their tents, it is the first care
of the women to conceal them during the season of riot and intoxication.*

Instructions for Turning Off

an advisory note for fur traders new to the continent

À la façon du pays. The custom of the country. French traders, British officers and company men, missionaries and Scottish clergy, visitors from Upper and Lower Canada – sate your sexual appetite with a Native woman.

> Use her as you wish:
> fuck her,
> impregnate her,
> make a home with her.
> Whatever.

If she's lucky, you'll feed and clothe her and your offspring. You'll return from your adventures to her bed. She's smart, she's strong, she knows ways to survive on the land, to make it through the winter. She'll help you negotiate, create trading ties – her words, like her body, currency. Her people aren't used to church weddings, so there's that, too.

Then turn her off.

You're assigned to another post, you're moving farther west, you don't want to be pinned down or you'd like a newer model. Leave her in the hands of another officer, a friend or a relative, toss in a dowry for good measure. Salve your conscience by sending money for the children.

Then, return to Scotland or to Upper Canada to your European wife.

Or stay here in Rupert's Land, trade up, find a white woman, an "exotic" who serves as a model of womanliness. She may be your cousin or half your age or both. Be like Chief Factor Donald McKenzie, colony governor in 1825. Find a white woman who's industrious, churchgoing – after all, as Donald says, "Nothing can give greater comfort to a husband than the satisfaction of having a wife who is nearly mute."

But be cautious. George, Governor Simpson, has advocated for the abolition of marriages of convenience – the same George who some claim has fathered eleven children, most by four different Native women; a man proud of his "bits of brown," who once claimed these alliances are "the best security we can have of the good will of the Natives."

Indeed, when he toured posts, Simpson wrote:

pray keep an eye on the
commodity. If she bring forth anything
in the proper time & of the right colour,
let them be taken care of but if
anything be amiss, let the whole
be bundled about their business.

The governor's new wife, eighteen to his forty-two, is an exotic he found in Scotland – his cousin, no less – and she will bring refinement to the colony, an air of "high life and gaiety," a delicate woman to whom he'll give a painted house, a carriole and a pianoforte.

But wait –

Simpson, who has travelled back home to find this morsel of virginal flesh, hasn't told Margaret Taylor, mother of his sons, one of whom is only six months old. No matter – George arranges for Amable Hogue, mason, to take Margaret, prompting one observer to write:

The Govrs little tit bit Peggy Taylor…is married to Amable Hogue…
what a downfall is here
…from a Governess to Sow.

And so, if you're planning to turn off your commodity,
a bit of notice is prudent.

People on the Stage

Letitia Hargrave, 1813–1854

Being a discourse on Indians by Letitia MacTavish Hargrave, white wife of James Hargrave. Letitia, whose husband arranged for a "weatherproof" piano to be shipped to York Factory and whom local Ininiwak women called Hockimaw Erqua, or female chieftain. Other names: diarist, social commentator, opiner on Red River society. In a note to her mother –

I only observed one or two ½ breeds, one was a woman the only female except ourselves and Mrs. Potter & Marg. She had a baby with her & its unhappy legs wrapt up in a moss bag. It looked like a mummy. I have not been near enough to inspect closely but I shall make Marg fetch a child over without the mother that I may examine it.

The moment it is born they get the bag stuffed with soft moss which has been in readiness & stuff the wretch into it up to the neck, bind it tightly round like a mummy, so as to make it as firm & flat as a deal board, then fasten it around their own back & work away about what they have to do. They don't mind the moss being wet & dirty but consider it a great convenience that they have no trouble shifting [it] at least for a long time.

The Indians all walk with their feet turned in from this discipline & their arms are as stiff as if there was not a joint in them. While the whites gentle and simple are running around perspiring with haste the Indians stalk along the platforms with their backs bent as if it were entirely for pleasure that they were wheeling barrows. They march so slowly & look so stately that they remind me of people on the stage.

Teacher

The teacher should be *more than Christian, she should be*
able to teach the ornamental arts, useful branches of education,
should be well-bred, able to teach music and drawing, be
of conciliating disposition and mild temper.

                              Send two
respectable English women, says Governor Simpson: *we consider*
it very desirable that the young ladies should have as little
discourse with the Native women in this country as possible.

Oh dear, a student, the daughter of Chief Trader Roderick
McKenzie Jr., has become pregnant – she's seduced a young
Indian – and so *the poor silly stupid creature must be married off.*
Chief Trader Ross puts his foot down. And soon *the ladies of this*
Academy are as strictly guarded as the inmates of a Turkish seraglio.

And so, within a year, with forty young women at the school,
a new governess – Widow Lowman, a clever, unsurpassed
woman. *She spares no pains with her pupils – she learns them to sit,*
to stand, to walk, and perhaps, to lie down. She appears to have their
improvement very much at heart – when she reprimands them, she does it
in the Kind affectionate terms of a Mother.

Oh, what's this?

Following the River

Our children's governess has changed both her name
and her condition – the Widow Lowman having become the current
Mrs. Bird. James Bird's country wife, Elizabeth, dead only three
months ago, and *Bird, that older shrivelled bag of dry bones*
has purchased this fresh morsel of frail humanity, soul
and body, for the sum of £2500, good and lawful money of
Great Britain, made over into her and her heirs forever

– an old man's lust, is surely "that worm that never dies."

A clever woman, fast rising to the top of the tree.
And soon, the mother of two more little Birds.

Polka Queen

Caroline Pruden, 1829–1908

The event of the year, the night filled with dance
and promise. Jigs, strathspeys and reels in one
room; gallops, valses, quadrilles and schottisches
in the other, and Caroline wants
                    to dance the polka.

Caroline, one of eleven children of John Peter
Pruden and Nancy Patasegawisk, who died before
her daughter began to dream of dresses and wraps
and carriages and balls. John Peter is stern –
daughter Charlotte had been with child at twelve;
it's difficult to raise girls without a mother.

But soon, the governess Ann Armstrong
is in his life, a pious woman who trails rumours
she'd slept with the captain on the voyage out
from England, and who, it is said, finds
the handsome John Peter vulgar and coarse,

unrefined – in truth, as Letitia Hargrave writes
in her diaries, the two are cat and dog on
either side of the hearth, one spattering, the other

snarling – but is anyone surprised? John is an old
Indian trader, and Ann is white, exotic, a catch for
a retired company man with a brood to raise.

And now this. Do tell!
         A ball at the fort, a night of protocol
and posturing, puffery and perfume, and Ann
and Caroline eager for a society turn. Not an event
to warm the heart of a codger.

In fairness, John Peter is not without flair. For
his new bride, he's brought from England a carriage
and a Dalmatian. On their twenty-five acres, they raise
geese, and one summer, a wild goose joins
the flock; every Sunday, as the carriage delivers
the Prudens to St. John's, the dog and the goose follow,
the Dalmatian trotting and the goose skipping and flapping.
They wait quietly by the carriage until the church service
is over. Years later, Caroline's friend Harriet speaks
of the animal, how its coat reminds her of spilled ink.
         Harriet, of course, always fond of novelty,

which brings us
back to the dance, an event at Fort Garry
in March of 1848 so remarkable more ink is shed,
in diaries and letters –

about a threesome, the belles of the ball: Misses Harriet
and Margaret Sinclair, Harriet sporting the first pair of white
kid gloves in Red River – brought by her father from
New York – and Caroline, the local beauty, envy of her friends,
who's been reading of the new dance from Bohemia.

"May I?" Caroline asks permission from her stepmother.
No harm trying, Ann apparently says; after all, she hopes
her stepdaughter will win over the beau monde; she's
taught her to speak, stand, dress, stay away from
"that quarter," the cruder girls of the colony.

Ann watches as the floor fills with exuberant
half-step spinning in four/four time, a closed-couple dance,
young bodies
                   well-nigh touching.
When Caroline's feet stop turning, when the music
falls away, a gruff voice from the sidelines shoots
through the crowd:

"Miss Disobedience! Come here!"

And Caroline, with her heart-shaped
face, wide-set eyes, loosened hair and glowing
cheeks, startles –

                   Oh, the shame.
The ball not nearly over,
but the night is. The Pruden women,
ordered to gather their wraps, are driven
home in the dark.

Tall Poppy: How to Write a Red River Tragedy

Sarah Ballenden, 1818–1853

1. Introduce the Main Characters and Set Them Up for Trouble

The trip from the officers' mess to the bedroom is short, it seems. Whispers: they're doing a bit of business, enjoying horizontal refreshment, amorous congress, knocking boots. They must be. She's one of the "blues," the elite of Red River, and he, Captain Foss, is a hotheaded Irish officer, new to Fort Garry, second in command of the Chelsea Pensioners.

She – the chief factor's wife – strolls from table to table, greeting regulars, welcoming visitors who stop off at the fort on their way west or north. Beautiful, charming, she's "a delightful creature," says Hargrave, dispensing approval from HBC offices at York Factory. A "creature" raised in Mackenzie trading posts, daughter of Chief Trader Alexander McLeod and an Indian woman. As a young girl, Sarah travels to Red River to finish school and, at eighteen, meets John, a young HBC clerk. A man with a future, Ballenden is, and after a stint for the company at the Soo, the two return to Red River, John as chief factor and Sarah as the highest ranking "half-breed" woman at the fort.

Where she meets Captain Christopher Foss.

Bright, vivacious, almost European in her manner, Sarah is the chatelaine of Fort Garry, hostess of grand parties, the belle of the colony. And now, a target.

2. Assemble Antagonists

Anne Clouston, who has travelled from Stromness to Rupert's Land, laden with so many trunks of finery Letitia Hargrave wonders if the woman thought she was coming to Calcutta. When Anne arrives in Fort Garry with her airs and frippery, she becomes a laughingstock.

On the same ship are David Anderson, newly appointed bishop of Rupert's Land, and his sister, sharp-tongued Margaret, who's come as his housekeeper, fiercely determined to protect her brother from Red River degeneracy and heathens who don't like the Church of England.

Waiting at York Factory is Augustus Pelly, accountant at Fort Garry. Once off the ship, the bishop hitches Anne Clouston to Augustus. Back at Fort Garry, Pelly loses money to Captain Foss, and worse, when Pelly's lust for Sarah is rebuked, he is humiliated. Salt in the wound: the captain and Sarah mock him over meat and potatoes in the mess hall.

Anglican Reverend William Cockran, who'd married Sarah and John Ballenden, isn't trusting the couple's Presbyterian leanings. Cockran and Ballenden have fought over a piece of land. And Reverend Cockran's wife – rumoured to have been a dollymop in England – prefers not to mix with the "duskier" women of Red River, especially those who rise above their station.

Chief Trader at Fort Garry, John Black, who wants Ballenden's job.

Fort Garry mess cook John Davidson and his English wife, who must suffer the indignity of working for Sarah Ballenden.

And there you have them:

The Pellys and the Andersons, the Cockrans and the Blacks, the Davidsons and, oh, let's not forget Major Caldwell (known as "an unmitigated ass"), who is Captain Foss's superior and miffed with him.

Imagine their chorus rising:

Sarah and the captain flirted: I saw them at the mess.
They laughed at Augustus! They mocked Anne!
I saw them behind the fort. They were meeting in secret.
Sarah's the kind of woman who isn't satisfied with a husband;
she wants a sweetheart too.
John Ballenden is entitled to a divorce. This is outrageous.

[But remember, Sarah has supporters, too:

She works hard, moves with grace and ease.
She holds parties with champagne!
She has named her daughter Frances after
Governor Simpson's wife, and is a friend
of Annie Bannatyne and other elites.
And hasn't Sarah been welcoming and generous?]

3. Introduce a Triggering Event

John Ballenden leaves Red River to meet Governor Simpson at Fort Alexander. Sarah is pregnant. The muckrakers' conclusion: Surely it is the captain's child.

Sarah is shunned. Captain Foss is furious.

Sarah asks her servant girl, Catherine Winegart, to sign a statement swearing she has seen no illicit behaviour between the captain and Mrs. Ballenden. It's not enough.

Captain Foss posts a notice on the front gates of the fort: no gossip about Mrs. Ballenden will be tolerated. (It wasn't his idea – lawyer and fort recorder Adam Thom suggested it).

The move backfires: the chinwagging and slander continue.

John Ballenden returns from Fort Alexander, and John Black (the one who wants Ballenden's job) presents Ballenden with a sworn deposition from the mess cook, Davidson, and his wife – they've been watching, and here's what's going on – and Ballenden – heartsick, confused, loyal to Sarah – wants only the truth.

4. Up the Ante

Captain Foss antagonizes the antagonists. He launches a charge of defamatory conspiracy against the Pellys and the Davidsons for accusing him of "criminal intercourse" with a married woman. He is determined to clear "the reputation of a Lady." The colony is up in arms.

The trial begins. Thom represents Sarah. He also sits on the bench. The jury is largely mixed-descent (who loathe Adam Thom, but Thom is on Sarah's side, so…).

The Reverend Cockran's wife takes the stand and perjures herself. Margaret Anderson, sister of the bishop, takes the stand and unleashes venom, laying bare her true character. Adam Thom takes the stand (counsel, judge and witness – somehow he is all three), and says:

"Mrs. Ballenden may not have as much 'starch' in her face as the white women of Red River, but she has as much virtue in her heart as any exotic."

Catherine Winegart, Sarah's servant, can't take the stand. She has left the settlement.

Adam Thom wins the case. The Pellys and the Davidsons are humiliated, forced to pay Captain Christopher Foss £300 in damages.

5. Make the Victory Pyrrhic

Red River divisions deepen. It's bluebloods against mixed bloods.

And Sarah is both.

6. Throw in Comic Relief: The French Farce Moment

By now, the colony has an acting governor-in-chief, Eden Colvile, who quickly has a spate of visitors.

Knock, knock.

It's Sarah and John Ballenden at the door.

Whoops. Bishop Anderson and his sister, Margaret, who arrived a few minutes ago, are in the other room.

(A smart pig gets to the market early.)

"I had to cram them into another room," says Colvile, "until the Bishop's visit was over…but he had to pass through this room. It was altogether like a scene in a farce."

Door. Door. Door. Slam. Slam. Slam.

7. Change the Setting, Move the Protagonists

John and Sarah move to the Lower Fort; Captain Foss stays in the Upper Fort. John's health deteriorates, and he travels to England for treatment. While John is gone, tongues sharpen again. Someone gives Adam Thom – the lawyer who defended Sarah – a letter written to Captain Foss from, it seems, Sarah. Thom shows it to Colvile who, of course, scrambles to show it to Governor Simpson.

My own darling Christopher, it begins.

The letter-writer asks the captain to come for a visit to the Lower Fort, where she will have a hot supper waiting for him.

A hot supper. Eden Colvile relishes this.

He writes:

The original having been delivered, the said darling Christopher came down & remained closeted in her rooms for two days and nights, but they managed matters so well, that to this hour, though it was of course known that Foss was absent from his own quarters, no one but Thom, myself, and the deliverer of the letter, whose name I cannot even tell you, have been able to prove that he was here.

8. Leave Unanswered Questions

Were Sarah and Captain Foss up to their old tricks? Did they commit adultery (as Jimmy Carter would one day do) only in their hearts? Were they set up? And did someone other than Sarah write the letter?

9. Bring the Story Home, Sad as It May Be

Captain Christopher Foss leaves Red River for good. Sarah gives birth to her eighth child, becomes ill; John returns from overseas, and when he is offered a post at Fort Vancouver, Sarah cannot join him.

Sarah spends the following winter in a house in the lower settlement near the rapids – John, Christopher and most of her allies gone. A friend later writes: *If there is such a thing as dying of a broken heart, she cannot live long.*

In 1852, Sarah and her children travel to Norway House, where Chief Factor George Barnston and his mixed-blood wife, Ellen Barnston, greet them warmly.

Ballenden, now critically ill, leaves Fort Vancouver for Scotland, sending word to have Sarah meet him in Edinburgh, where he can retire. The two reunite only briefly.

On December 23, 1853, Sarah dies in Scotland of consumption.

She is thirty-five.

10. Write a Coda: A Story is Never Over

In a letter to his daughter Annie – around fifteen years old when her mother dies – John Ballenden writes:

Following the River

Mrs. Barnston is my very good friend. She was the earliest, best and most constant friend of your own dear mother. On arrival at the Lower Fort you will wait there until I have the pleasure of meeting you. From thence I will conduct you to the Upper Fort, and once here it will not be my fault if ever again we are separated. I have no intention of sending you again to school.

I cannot part with you yet.

Sally (Sarah) Erasmus Kennedy

Sally (Sarah) Erasmus Kennedy – Devoted Labourer –
Dusky Worshippers – Oayache Mannin – Travels with Harriet –
Backbiters – Woman with a Backbone – Mama is an Indian –
Elizabeth Setter Norquay – Maria Thomas: Infernal Liar

Sally (Sarah) Erasmus Kennedy

b. circa 1830 (St. Andrews) – d. 1889 (South Dufferin)

Sally, Kitty's daughter
and Catherine's mother,
born 1830 or '31 in Red River,
                one mention of you
as a young woman, in your brother
Peter's memoir:
you and your sister preparing
a meal on his return to St. Andrews
after years away. You are married
to Antoine Kennedy by then,
member of the Peguis Nation.

In 1854, Antoine's and your name appear
in the list of the first 127 communicants
in the new stone church.

So many babies – more
than the census shows.
Eight in fourteen years,
half of whom live
less than a year.

Following the River

(Yet Catherine will
tell her own daughter she
had no siblings.)

Antoine, almost twenty years
your senior, a carpenter
according to the census,
a tripman according to other
sources. One of Henry Prince's men.

In 1880, your sister Mary Anne
is in Prince Albert, along with
your mother, Kitty, and your son John.
Would they have fled to Saskatchewan
with other Métis after the resistance?
Your brother Peter travelled farther,
to Alberta.

In 1882, *man sick* recorded
on the Peguis band pay sheet.

In 1883, *man dead.*
That year, you apply to the Indian
agent for help settling Antoine's estate.
By 1889, you too are gone, separated
from the land you farmed, your home
for fifty years. What children remain
are off into lives of their own.

Clandeboye Man.
22d September 1883

Sir/

I have the honor to laying
before you the case of Mrs Antoine
Kennedy, widow of Antoine Kennedy
both Indians of St Peters Band.

Antoine Kennedy died a short
time ago. leaving a widow, one son. who
does not take the treaty and who lives
at Prince Albert, and three daughters,
two of whom are married to non Treaty
men and one to an Indian.

Mrs Kennedy called on me and
wants her husband's estate settled, there
are two River lots in all 11 chains
frontage by two Miles. Six head of
Animals 3 Pigs. a mower. Plough. Harrows. Carts &c. — The daughter who married the Indian received when she
married five chains of land an ox-
a cow & calf as her share, The son
the mother states received his share
from her husband before he went
to Prince Albert.

J. P. Wright Esq.   The
   Indian Office
      Winnipeg
         Man

Correspondence regarding the estate of Antoine Kennedy of St. Peter's
Reserve (Clandeboye Agency). Indian Affairs (RG 10, Volume 3657,
File 9129), Online Mikan No. 2061431, www.collectionscanada.gc.ca

Devoted Labourer

Sophia Thomas Mason, 1822–1861

The Lord is my strength and my shield [Psalm 28:7]

Pleurisy, the English climate, yet daily Sophia sits at the desk,
translating one word at a time. By 1859, she's completed
the New Testament. By 1861, the Old.
                    England is a long way from Red River
and Sophia no longer the twenty-one-year-old so well schooled
she'd been offered the position of governess in the academy. Her father,
Governor Dr. Thomas, and his country wife have raised a bright
young woman to thrive in colony society, related as she is to
two chief factors, as well as Governor Simpson's first country wife.

I shall not want [Psalm 23:1]

Only six when her father dies, Sophia is taken in by
Reverend David Jones, who is soon off to England, leaving her with
Reverend Cockran. Fluent in Cree, and scholarly, Sophia turns down
the position at Red River Academy to wed William Mason,
a young Methodist missionary, and they travel to Norway House,
unaware they are pawns in one of Governor Simpson's machinations:
to slow down the southern migration to Red River, bring religion
to the Natives of Norway House and its nearby settlement, Rossville.

Blessed are the meek [Matthew 5:5]

Not Church Missionary Society, and not Catholic, but Methodists,
the lowliest of faiths, yet enough God to sop the spiritual needs
of the Cree.

And, says Simpson to Chief Factor Donald Ross, to tamp
down the actions of James Evans, flouter of HBC rules,
founder of the nearby Rossville mission, supporter of free trade
and a man rumoured to have bedded three maidens and driven
a few others in his carriole to the ends of roads where there are
no houses. Evans, who has begun, with the local Ininiwak,
to develop Cree syllabics,
and is working with Sophie and William to translate the Bible.

For in the day of trouble He will conceal me [Psalm 27:5]

Evans wants no work on Sundays, wants support for the
starving in Rossville, wants more than the governor is ready
to grant. As Ross, Simpson, Evans and Mason busy themselves
with territorial tugs-of-war, Sophia works fervently, translating
hymns and scripture for services, visiting mission tents
and teaching.

For where your treasure is, there your heart will be also [Matthew 6:21]

Sophia is diligent:
"Most people deem the cares of a family quite enough to employ
the time of a female," writes her husband. Words are her mission.
All that, writes William, "in the wilderness, where, in time of sickness,
no medical assistance could be procured." Soon James Evans is gone,

a heart attack in England, and William, suspected busybody and
instigator of salacious rumours, abandons the Methodists
and takes up a post in York Factory with the Church of England.

Take nothing for the journey [Luke 9:3]

The Bible will be printed. Sophia and William bring
the translations across to England to oversee the work.
Weak with pleurisy, Sophia is rigorous, conscientious, tireless,
the passages draining her strength, but, at long last,
it is complete, collected, published, and there, inside the front cover,
are listed the names of the translators:

William Mason and two
Cree men – Reverend Steinhauer and John Sinclair.

For Thine is the kingdom, the power and the glory [Matthew 6:13]

Sophia dies soon after. She is thirty-nine. In 1861, the *Church Missionary
Gleaner* publishes "A short sketch of the life and Missionary labours
and happy death of Sophia Mason."

       "Oh, how great is my loss and that of the nine
poor orphan children," writes William in despair. "She has been spared
to accomplish a great work, the Cree Bible, and to bear such a testimony
for Jesus amongst the heathen." Her perfect command and knowledge
of the Indian language: "invaluable."

Fulsome words.

Let us turn now to 2 Corinthians 4:18: *So we fix our eyes not on what is seen, but on what is unseen. For what is seen is temporary, but what is unseen is eternal.*

In the beginning was the Word.
Sophia's last is *heaven.*

Dusky Worshippers

Testamentum by Henry Youle Hind (1823–1908), explorer and author, on his experience in the stone church, October 4, 1857:

A fair proportion of the congregations come to and go
from church in neat carriages, or on horseback,
and the external appearance of the assemblages, taken

as a whole, in relation to dress, is superior to what we are
accustomed to see in Canada, or in the country parishes
of Great Britain. The young men wear handsome blue cloth

frock coats with brass buttons, and 'round their waist, a long
scarlet woollen sash; the young women are neatly dressed
like the country girls at home, but in place of a bonnet

they wear the far more becoming shawl or coloured
handkerchief thrown over or tied 'round the head;
sometimes they allow their long black hair to serve

the purpose of a covering and ornament, for which, from
its profusion, it is admirably fitted. In this particular, many
of the half-breed girls follow the custom of their Indian

ancestry, who, as a general rule, never cover the head.
The church at the Indian settlement is also a new, spacious
building of stone, with a wall of the same material enclosing

the churchyard, in which is a wooden schoolhouse, where
I saw about fifty Ojibway Indian young men, young women
and children receiving instructions from the Reverend

A. Cowley, Mrs. Cowley and a Native schoolmaster. The young
Indian women read the Testament in soft, low voices, but
with ease and intelligence. During service, the church

was almost three-fourths full. The congregation appeared to be
exclusively Indian; in their behaviour, they were most decorous
and attentive. The singing was very sweet, and all the forms of

the service appeared to be understood, and practised quietly
and in order by the dusky worshippers. A seraphino was played
by Mrs. Cowley to accompany the singers; responses were well

and exactly made, and the utmost attention was given to
the sermon. The prayers were read in English, the lessons
in Ojibway, and the sermon was delivered in Cree. After service

an Indian child, neatly dressed in white, was baptized. A few of
the women and girls wore bonnets, but the greater number drew
their shawls over the head. A wonderful contrast, the subdued

Indian worshippers in this missionary village present on Sunday
to the heathen revellers of the Prairies, who perform their
disgusting ceremonies within a mile and a half of some of

Following the River

the Christian altars of Red River. On two Sundays during my visit,
at the time when Divine service was being celebrated in all
the churches of the settlement, the heathen Indians held

their dog feasts and medicine dances on the open plain.

Oayache Mannin

Watch how the shadows sway, fling themselves up toward
the rafters and drop, how they gather everyone in. How a hearth
of packed mud and hay rises along the back, and beneath it, out of
a pan of grease with a cotton rag wick, leaps an unsteady, lapping flame.
Notice the four-poster bed, a chair or two, but they are empty:

everyone – women, children, old men – sitting on the plank floor.
All but the spirited fiddler, and all but the dancers who move into
the centre, draw back, their moccasins light and nimble on the wood,
fancy steps, arranged like words, telling the crowd where they are from.
Le gigue du bas Canada – the jig on the Red.

One night, they say, a Scot played his pipes;
across the river, Métis overheard,
took up a fiddle to mimic the sound, double the time.

Ho! Ho! And here we go now:
Back step four times, and front four times. Double. Front step four
times. Single. Triple tap four times. Triple tap, accent right. Triple tap,
accent left. Heel, toe. And more to go. A black-eyed beauty in blue calico
and a strapping Bois-Brûlé. Heels *thump thumping*, shadows skittering.
A baby whirls in the arms of her sister; an old woman at the edge of
the circle folds her shawl over her heart, looks down as her soft-shoe

Following the River

steps lean into a twirl. Light flares, the dancers speed up, draw back, heel, toe, cross arms.

Ho! Ho! The fiddle yelps: a devil at the bow.

Travels with Harriet

Harriet Goldsmith Sinclair Cowan (1832–1926), granddaughter of William Sinclair and Nahoway

1856. To Moose Fort. Twelve hundred miles in four weeks, with two young children. We went from Fort Garry in a large canoe – a canot du nord, as it was called, about thirty feet long, light and wonderfully strong. It had a wooden grating on the bottom to protect the birchbark.

We had buffalo robes and blankets for our bedding, tarpaulins to shield us from the rain. In bad weather, the tarpaulins were stretched over the tents at our camping places. Our luggage and supplies had to be as light as possible. We had a large kettle, a frying pan and a teakettle, all of iron, for ourselves, and the men had the same. The men had flint and steel and touchwood. My husband had wax vestas, which we used to get from England in tin boxes. One of the men was also the cook; the men cooked for themselves.

We took with us a couple of wicker trunks. Our heavy trunks and other heavy things were sent up to York Factory to be taken in the company's ship to England and brought back to us across the Atlantic next year by the ship coming to Moose Factory. Our canoe, which had a crew of eight men, took us down the Red to Lake Winnipeg, across to Fort Alexander at the mouth of the Winnipeg River and up that river more than two hundred miles, with its many falls and rapids, which meant many portages.

We crossed Lac Seul or Lac Sal (it is known by both names), a long lake that is like the Thousand Islands portion of the St. Lawrence, and on

to the height of land, and after that travelled by many lakes and streams. We hoisted sail whenever we had a favouring wind. From Martin's Falls, we went three hundred miles down the Albany River in smooth, swift water all the way to its mouth on James Bay, where we came to Fort Albany. Then we left our canoe and went the hundred miles from Fort Albany, the saltwater part of our travelling, in an open boat along the coast to Moose Factory, or Moose Fort as it was usually called.

In that part of James Bay, it is shallow, and when the tide is out, unless there is a wind from the north, the water is so far away from the shore as to be out of sight. On the first evening, when the men were rowing towards a place where we thought we might camp for the night, the boat grounded and was left high and dry by the tide, which went out rapidly because there was an offshore wind. Some of the men walked the long distance to shore, scrambling over the rocks and through the mud, and brought back firewood and made a fire on the rocks near our boats to boil our kettle, and after supper, we made ourselves as comfortable as we could to await the turning of the tide. Fortunately, there was not a wind to bring back the water in a rush.

On our way to the mouth of the Moose River, we saw several white whales and many seals. And when at last we came to Moose Fort, which like Fort Albany is on an island at the mouth of the river, I thought it a delightful place.

1863. Return to Fort Garry. It took us longer to come back over that twelve hundred miles, chiefly because of the hard, heavy work in tracking up the Albany river, when the men had to haul the canoe against the current. Before we started from Moose Fort, we arranged to have our trunks and heavy boxes taken by the company's ship to England and brought out the next year to York Factory, and from there brought down to Fort Garry.

We left Moose Fort on July 8 in wet weather. I was wearing long, waterproof Eskimo moccasins of sealskin up to my knees. We arrived at Fort Garry on September 8. The crew of Indians who brought us from Fort

Albany to Lac Seul would come no farther. They were afraid of the Indians they would meet on this side of the height of land.

We had to wait at Lac Seul three days until the Indians who were to bring us on to Fort Garry arrived. There was only one man among them who had ever been to Fort Garry, and that was twenty years before. I remember I was at first a little afraid, but we soon found that they were very good-natured. They would travel for miles to find a good place for the camp at night, and would cut brush and go to great trouble to make everything comfortable for the children and me. Indeed, they were very kind to us.

The heat and monotony in such weather were trying for the children. The Indians used to show them how to weave rushes. They did everything they could to please the children and keep them amused. When we got back to Red River, the children and I stayed a while at my uncle Thomas Sinclair's house at the rapids.

1864. To England, to leave our three children there to be educated. Seven hundred miles to York Factory, on Hudson Bay, by the Red River, Lake Winnipeg and the Nelson.

We arrived at York Factory on the evening the company's ship Prince of Wales *came to anchor, after suffering injury from running on a reef near Mansfield Island. Her sister ship, the* Prince Arthur, *was lost on the same reef. A small chartered ship, the* Ocean Nymph, *which had crossed with the two company ships and had kept clear of the reefs, took the crew of the* Prince of Wales *and the survivors from the* Prince Arthur *back to England, and we went on her. There were sixty people on board. The* Ocean Nymph *was a small ship, and rolled dreadfully, and as she was overcrowded with passengers on that voyage, we really had a most uncomfortable time of it between the decks in bad weather.*

A little girl was buried at sea. She was the daughter of an officer of the company who had retired and was going home to the Orkneys with his wife, an Indian woman, and their only child. Several retired company men who had married women of Indian or mixed descent had taken them home to the Orkneys. I have never forgotten that funeral at sea and the grief of the mother of the child.

1865. The voyage outward from London to Rupert's Land. When my husband and I went on board the Prince Rupert at Stromness the following June, we found the ship a delightful contrast to the Ocean Nymph. There was accommodation for cabin passengers and for steerage passengers. Each state room had an upper and a lower berth. The meals were excellent. There were cows on board to provide milk, and there were pigs and sheep and poultry. Really, we lived luxuriously. I remember that before we left Stromness, great quarters of fine Orkney beef were drawn high up on the masts and fastened there. The surface became hardened by the wind and the sun, and beneath it, the meat kept perfectly fresh during the voyage.

While we were crossing Davis Strait, a crow's nest was hoisted to the top of the main mast. It was a large cask, open at the top with a trap door in the bottom, and one of the sailors kept a lookout for the ice, and they rigged up a bridge across the middle of the ship for the officer of the watch to be on while he was giving directions as we were going through the ice. Also, they got out fenders and long poles with spikes, and ice anchors too, for mooring the ship to the ice when that was necessary.

We were seventeen days fast in the ice of the strait. Another ship of the company's that was with us, the Lady Head, was icebound about half a mile from us. The captain of the Lady Head, the ship that went every year to Moose Fort, invited us to dinner one day, and persuaded us to stay for supper, to which we were just sitting down when there came a cry, "The ice is moving!" We had to hurry back to our own ship. Before we could get back on board the Prince Rupert, they had to put down a ladder so that we could cross the open water in a wide crack in the ice.

As for me, I thought the fog worse than either the storms or the ice. We had fine weather crossing the bay. The nights, I remember, were beautiful. When we were about fifty miles off Churchill, a couple of cannons were shot off on the chance that the reports might be heard by the Churchill schooner and so let them know that we were passing on our way to York Factory. As we came near the end of our voyage, we got a faint smell of spruce from the land, though the low shoreline was invisible. When we anchored at last in York Roads, twenty miles from the factory, only the high beacon twelve miles away on the point between the Nelson and the Hayes Rivers was visible from our ship. During the day, a cannon was fired at intervals to let them know on shore that we had come, and at night, rockets were sent up from the ship.

The next morning about nine o'clock, the schooner and the boats came in sight. The mail and the official documents were taken to York Factory, and the gunpowder, the dangerous part of the cargo – there were many tons of it – was transferred to the schooner and the boats, which had crews of rowers. Then the Prince Rupert moved into shallower water and anchored about seven miles from York Factory. When our guns were fired now, we could hear the guns at the factory reply. The next day, we sailed to the factory in the schooner.

We got to York Factory in September, then on to Norway House and wintered there.

Altogether, I have been across the bay and through Hudson Strait three times, and each time we were unfortunate in missing the Eskimos. When I was at Moose Fort, I used to see Eskimos quite frequently. The missionaries had a number of them at the Peel River Mission on the other side of James Bay, which was regular Eskimo country. The Eskimos we saw at Moose Fort were always chewing pieces of walrus ivory to shape them into beads for necklaces.

1870. It was in July that my husband and I, who were then living at the stone fort, made our preparations for escape. Governor McTavish had prevailed upon Riel to let us move down there. My husband went up to Fort Garry two or three times a week; I never knew whether he would be allowed to come back. Mounted men were stationed near the stone fort by Riel. When we had all our preparations made and a York boat landed, we started off for Lake Winnipeg as fast as our crew could row.

Following the River

One of Riel's mounted men galloped off to Fort Garry to tell him of our escape, but before we could be overtaken, we were out on the lake and on our way northward to York Factory.

Backbiters

Testamentum on a visit from the East, November 1868, by Canadian
journalist and poet Charles Mair (1838–1927):

After putting up at the Dutchman's Hotel
I went over and stayed at Dr. Schultz's
after a few days. The change was comfortable,
I assure you, from the racket of a motley crowd

of half-breeds, playing billiards and drinking,
to the quiet and solid comfort of a home.
Altogether I received hospitalities to my heart's
content, and left the place thoroughly pleased
with most I had met.

There are jealousies and heart-burnings, however.

Many wealthy people are married to half-breed
women who, having no coat of arms but a totem
to look back to, make up for the deficiency
by biting at the backs of their "white" sisters.

Following the River

The white sisters fall back upon
their whiteness, whilst the husbands meet
each other with desperate courtesies
and hospitalities, a view to filthy
lucre in the background.

Woman with a Backbone

Annie McDermot Bannatyne (1832–1908)

Annie has a backbone. And a whip.

She is born into wealth – both her father and her future husband, Andrew Bannatyne, are successful merchants. Annie is gracious and well liked, holds splendid dinner parties and is admired for her handsome appearance and elegant clothing. She is a benefactor; some say she's responsible for the Winnipeg General Hospital.

Annie will outlive seven of her ten children.

After reading an article by Charles Mair in an Ontario newspaper in 1868, Annie orders the clerk at her husband's store to let her know when Mair arrives on Saturday to collect his newspapers.

St. Boniface priest George Dugas writes later:

At four in the afternoon, while the store was full of people, Daniel Mulligan, the clerk, having seen Mair's arrival, ran to tell Mrs. Bannatyne. She quickly throws a shawl on her head and bursts into the post office, holding a large whip in her hand. Without hesitating, she advances on Mair, seizes his nose between her fingers and gives him five or six strokes of the whip on different parts of his body. "Look," she says, "this is how the women of Red River treat those who insult them." The scene lasted only half a minute...by evening, the incident was known all across the country.

Following the River

Annie's husband, Andrew Bannatyne, supports Louis Riel. After Andrew dies, Annie moves, some sources say, to Cannington Manor, a small experimental settlement in Saskatchewan built on Victorian values. The village nearby has a general store, a dairy and a blacksmith. Nearby residents can enjoy plays in the town hall, a poetry group, literary readings and more. There is some mystery there, however, as Cannington Manor is abandoned by the time Annie dies.

The manor is a fitting place for a forward-thinking woman, a place to talk literature and politics, including the likes of the arrogant *chien de mer* of years ago. Louis Riel's poem "At Oak Point" would have been an evening's entertainment.

In it, Annie lives on.

Let's put out to dry
La-i-tou-tra-la! Bis.
Let's put out to dry
The noses of the sea dog
Over there!!!

It's a lady that will show us
La-i-tou-tra-la! Bis.
It's a lady that will show us
How we should treat them
Over there!!!

Mama is an Indian

Jemima Ross (1837–1867)

We take up three of the six pews at the front, James.

Yes, we do – we're a big family.

After church, I heard someone comment on this. He said our brother-in-law must feel ashamed when he steps into the pulpit.

Of what?

Of all the black relations he must look at.

Our mother is an Indian. John is married to our sister. Why would he be ashamed of any of his flock?

I love mama, but I'm not sure I want her to come to church with us anymore.

Because she's an Indian?

Well, it's –

Who is more tender-hearted? More attached to her children and more desirous of their happiness? More attentive to their wants – anxious about their welfare?

Yes. But she…it's how she dresses, her –

Because she isn't accomplished in etiquette and fussy nonsense?

People stare at her, James. They talk.

Give me my mama over the cold-hearted so-called lady who prides herself in her fine shape and her clever but foolish jesting. Her superficials and secondaries of writing and hair-brushing and gait and posture.

Elizabeth Setter Norquay

b. 1843 – d. 1933

the daughter –

Imagining George Setter as he rouses the older children, stirs ashes in the fireplace, adds another length of white poplar, watches until the flames start up again. Isabella has been gone for a couple of years. He is the first one up now, Caroline and John James still in their bedrooms, awake but rustling.

The snow is flying about, and he places his fingers on the stretched hide where a nick lets the cold air spool in. Two ploughs and two harrows, more than others in the area, but no money for a proper glass pane, not yet. Before she died, his wife, Isabella, was the one to notice these things.

The shape of St. Andrews Church across the road is barely visible.

As he rummages in the cupboard for the children's lunch, his breath is a white cloud. The fire isn't catching well. There is enough bannock, at least. He wraps pieces and sets them on the table. As he puts on his coat, he turns back to call his youngest, Elizabeth.

"I'm headed out to the barn with your brother and sister," he might say to her. "Those calves won't feed themselves. This time ask John James to help you with the milk. We can't afford to lose any."

As the door closes, Elizabeth steps out of her bedroom carrying her outdoor clothes, sits down in front of the fire. The floor is covered in what everyone calls Indian mats, woven rushes dyed by the women up near Netley Creek, some of them relatives of her mother's. She wraps the duffels made of blue blanket-cloth from her moccasins up to her knees and ties them as best she can. Caroline will help tighten them.

She envies the girls who have garters. Next is the hand-me-down coat made of two-point blanket, its leather cord wrapped around her waist to keep out the cold and wind. Then hat and mittens.

It's still dark when the four return from the barn an hour later. First prayers and then the oatmeal her father often leaves on the stove for days, looking even stickier today than usual. "The legacy of the Orkneys," Elizabeth will say when she is an old woman. In a few years, her father will marry again, and by then she and her sister, Caroline, will be doing all the cooking.

the student –

But now, picking at the glutinous lump of oatmeal, she is thinking only of a friend's humiliation.

"Mr. Garrioch has no more slate pencils," she says.

"Where's yours? Did you lose it?" Her father hands her the bannock and she promptly stuffs it inside her coat. This batch had berries, saskatoons, so there was that to look forward to.

"No, I still have mine. But one of the Kennedy children had to use clay."

"That'll do, won't it?" Her father is always practical.

"It scratched the slate, and Mr. Garrioch wasn't happy."

"Let's go." John James has opened the door and snow is blowing into the room. "Let's go – they're here."

Elizabeth finishes cleaning her bowl and grabs her bag. "I'm going to Margaret's house after. Her mother has a lot of wool that needs teasing."

Her sister scowls. "But we still have to finish the knocking."

Caroline is always keeping people organized. Knocking isn't easy.

Barley is poured into a large bowl her father has crudely fashioned from wood, and then Caroline and Elizabeth take turns pounding it with a mallet while the other turns the barley to make sure all the grain is separated from the hulls. This year there was so much of it Elizabeth thought they'd never finish. She isn't as strong as Caroline, and John James won't do it. Woman's work, he calls it.

"Tomorrow, I promise."

Caroline squints at her.

The snow bites Elizabeth's face as she climbs into the carriole. Usually they walk, but on stormy days, Mr. Sinclair gives them a ride. We can imagine Elizabeth poking her feet down under the front seat, the hot stone meant to keep them warm already cooling. At school, more Bible reading. They take their places at their desks, boards sloped against the walls.

It was John James's task yesterday to make sure the boards were clean. And today it's Elizabeth who is chosen to hand out the alphabet cards to the younger children. The wood stove in the centre of the room makes the air so dry her hair lifts as she moves about. Today the ink in the goose-quill pens is not frozen, but Elizabeth will help with adding water to the dark powder – it is used up so fast. Usually after lunch they head outdoors to play cross-tag or wolf or button, button. But today too much snow flies about. Mr. Sinclair brought an old buffalo robe to the school the other day. Perhaps today is the day they can drag it over to the riverbank and use it as a toboggan. If they can see that far.

the wife –

In 1862, Elizabeth Setter marries John Norquay at Portage la Prairie. Elizabeth is twenty and John, a schoolteacher, twenty-one. Like so many others, their marriage is held on a Wednesday morning and followed by three days of dancing. On the following Sunday, as is the custom, the couple attends church – a coming out of sorts.

They live simply.

When drought and a grasshopper plague hit the region, they live on fish alone. Big John, well-schooled, serves as representative for the community of St. Andrews, then rises to the office of Premier of Manitoba in 1878. He is still called Junior, except by legislative council member Donald Gunn, who calls Norquay "Greasy John." A man of three hundred pounds, John has a soft, resonant voice and can speak many languages. Canadians and Métis both tend to trust him – he knows how to navigate rough waters.

He supports Riel's aims. Five years after Riel's death, John dies of appendicitis, too young, and Elizabeth, widow for forty-four years, will wear a brooch with a miniature photograph of John to the end of her days. Together, they raise eight children, five sons and three daughters, the youngest of whom, Ada, dies at the age of two.

the widow –

When a man named Healy comes to visit Mrs. Norquay, now in her nineties, Elizabeth reminisces about the land, takes him for a walk in the fields at St. Andrews to show him wild potato – aski-pawah – and wild turnip that Scottish settlers searched for in times of famine; red willow, known as kinikinick, the spring tonic; and the sap of the white spruce, the cure Natives used for scurvy.

Elizabeth knows how to make rubaboo, a mixture of boiled vegetables and pemmican, and rowshow, a pan-fried pancake of shredded pemmican and flour. She knows the land, knows Native ways, but what she knows or believes during the troubles is a mystery.

The year after Riel travels north to support Gabriel Dumont and the Saskatchewan Métis, the May 29, 1885, edition of *Portage La Prairie Weekly Tribune* reports:

Following the River

Hon. Mr. Norquay and Mrs. Norquay arrived in the Portage on Monday. Mr. Norquay returned to the metropolis on Tuesday, but Mrs. Norquay will remain in the town the guest of Sheriff Setter for two or three weeks.

Sheriff Setter: Elizabeth's brother John James – a supporter at heart of the Canadians. Supporters are rewarded.

For Batoche, General Middleton is knighted, given $20,000 by the Canadian government.

Do John and Elizabeth talk of this?

And soon, the area Elizabeth has known since childhood has grown tenfold in population. Her siblings are gone, and the woods along the river are filling with the houses of Anglo-Protestants. Soon Elizabeth's and John's heritage will be the mark of shame.

Long after Elizabeth dies, the Manitoba government proposes a plaque to commemorate John's service to Manitoba – he is the first Métis to serve as premier – but the descendants of John and Elizabeth threaten legal action unless references to his background are removed.

Maria Thomas: Infernal Liar

b. 1845 – d. 1867

The dress is French merino wool with lace on the sleeves, a treasure
for a young servant girl. In the house, in the barn and in the bushes
off the track, they say, Reverend Corbett stopping the carriage
when he feels the urge. The loft of the barn – a bunghole with
a view to his house. "Lie with me," he orders.

Corps bête, many Métis call the reverend. The beast.
A forty-year-old married Protestant minister, back in Red River
after a quick study of medicine in England. Corbett loathes
French Catholics, fancies himself a champion of English half-breeds
and now the victim of an outrageous miscarriage of justice.

Hadn't he taken thirteen-year-old Maria Thomas, half-breed
daughter of a mere tripman, into his house as a servant?

And this, this is the result?

A miscarriage: unfortunate word choice. Corbett has used
several means to miscarry the child Maria carries. But Maria
and her parents, Simon and Catherine Thomas,
                              will not back down.

The charges: rape and attempted abortion in the
General Quarterly Court of Assiniboia, 24 & 25 Vict. c. 100.

∾

Court is in session.

Five charges including the use of "a certain poison...a certain instrument or piece of wire, tied with tape to the forefinger of his right hand and with the point of the wire projecting about half an inch or three-quarters of an inch beyond the point of his said finger...in the direction of the os uteri...

further the said Griffith Owen Corbett, with the like intent to procure the miscarriage...did, on or about the 25th of June, one thousand eight hundred and sixty-two, at Mapleton aforesaid, thrust one of his hands, after he had rubbed it with oil, into and up her vagina or private parts toward and in the direction....
                         contrary to the form of the statute in such case made and provided, and against the peace of the Queen, her Crown and dignity..."

Nine days of testimony. On the stand –

Maria's mother, Catherine Thomas:

Mr. C. came into the room and took me and Maria and Mrs. C. into another room. I saw John Taylor with a paper, and he read it to us, and told Maria to repeat after him, which she did. He [Mr. C] gave Maria a vial and some pills, with directions how to use this medicine. She took the liquid from this vial. The liquid was like brandy and stained her mouth

and spoon. When the liquid was done, she took the pills, and continued doing so some time, but they purged her very violently.
Mrs. Leask said we were killing Maria by using them, and we threw them into the fire. Maria became very weak after leaving Mr. C. the last time. I was obliged to bathe her every night.

John Taylor, magistrate:

I brought the paper to make Maria swear. Maria then said if she had known what the paper contained she would not have consented to sign it.

Curtis James Bird, Doctor:

The effect of the medicine argote [sic] of rye: it is sufficient to cause abortion. My opinion is that the wire and finger were to produce abortion.

Joseph Berston, former employee of Corbett:

I have often seen them talking together out of doors, and in the byre. There was a loft in the byre made of rails, and hay on the top. There was no loft in the stable, but there was hay there. I could see marks in the hay in the stable as if someone had been sleeping or reclining on it. Saw the track once of a carriole and horse which had been stopping at the stable door.

Oliver Gowler, farmer:

I went up to the loft of Mr. C's stable to look for the hole I had heard Maria state at Mapleton that Mr. C. had made there to look towards his dwelling house. There was a hole, and it had been bunged up with mud.

Following the River

Henry Cochrane, Reverend:

Mr. Corbett requested me to speak to Maria. He wished me to advise her to remain and marry J. Chamberlain.

The Venerable Hunter, Archdeacon:

I know Maria Thomas, and saw her before legal steps had been taken against Mr. Corbett, because Simon Thomas had lain a complaint against Mr. C. that Mr. C. had got his daughter with child. I went down on the 24th. I found her in bed. She told me she was with child by Mr. C. I warned her to be careful of what she was saying: "As a Minister of God, he will put you and your whole family into prison."

Simon Thomas, Maria's father:

He, Mr. C., wished me to get my daughter, Maria, married to J. Chamberlain, and said he would give her half his lot: the upper side. He left at half past six o'clock. Before we went to take a walk, I went into my house with him. I went out, and while I was outside – and while there – heard a cry from my child. I knew it to be Maria's voice. When I went inside of my house after I heard the cry, I saw nothing. At first I could not get in. When I got in, I saw Mr. C. bathing his hands. Maria told me she was in the family way.

Mr. James Ross, journalist and counsel:

Gentlemen, this is no ordinary trial. A clergyman of very high social position and hitherto unblemished character is the person accused – and the crime charged is one of the most degrading and revolting in the whole criminal calendar.

Utter ruin stares my client in the face if the allegations of Maria Thomas and her family are to be credited. He will become an outcast – his own peace and that of his family will be forever destroyed – his name, it will be a byword – and his future will be fraught only with misery and degradation.

Is this a result, gentlemen, which you are prepared to entail upon the prisoner on such confused and contradictory evidence? Will you assume the responsibility of ruining a fellow man upon the testimony of a lying girl, supported by a mother and a sister whose veracity is as questionable as Maria's virtue was easy?

∾

The Verdict in the Street –

Maria Thomas has been walking alone, wearing the wrong clothes for the occasion, speaking to people beyond her station, displaying gifts she has received from the reverend.

She knows too much about sexual matters from the book the reverend has shown her.

It's unbefitting. Corbett is being framed.

His fault lies in challenging the HBC, and the company employs Maria's father, Simon – this is political. Maria is not innocent – she has given birth to his child.

The Verdict in Court –

Corbett is convicted, not of rape but of attempted abortion.
His supporters free him from jail.

∾

Within the year, Corbett returns to England alone, where he becomes a curate in several small parishes. Rumours begin of illicit goings-on, and he is forced to quit.

Maria dies young, the fate of her infant child undetermined.

Catherine Kennedy Couture

Catherine Kennedy Couture – Patient Wife – Upright: Or,
Intelligence Comes to Red River – The Girl Who Loved You
So True – Invisible – Enfranchise – Town Kisser – Where They
Cannot Find Her: May 12, 1885 – Doing Laundry in the Resistance –
Sister Annie Goulet – The Indian Question: What Settler
Women Say – Don't Spoil Your Looks – All the Names –
Once Upon a Bird – Klondike Kitty: Sarah Ann
Catherine Couture – "I am on way home" – This Moon

Catherine Kennedy Couture

b. 1858 – d. 1908

Baptized February 13, 1859,
fourth daughter of Antoine Kennedy, carpenter,
    and Sally (Sarah) Kennedy. Great-grandmother.

The year you are born, Chief Peguis and pro-Canada
forces have begun discussions that will result
in Treaty 1. Buffalo are now scarce. "Canadian" coins are
minted, although the British sovereign continues to be
legal tender. Chinese immigrants have begun settling
in parts of what will become Canada. Gold, discovered on
the Thompson River a year before, starts the Fraser
Canyon Gold Rush.

Macy's department store opens in New York.
Hymen Lipman patents the first pencil with an eraser attached.
Puccini is born.

The Second Opium War is underway – a resistance
to Britain's goal of dominating the opium trade as well as
opening all of China to British merchants.

Following the River

When you are two years old, the first Canadian
postage stamps are printed.

The year you are nine, Canada becomes a country.

The following year, grasshoppers descend,
and their bodies are piled four feet high around
Fort Garry walls. Years of insect infestation follow,
cause the Canadian government to pledge funds to
support the starving, funds that went sideways,
used instead to build a road to Lake Superior.

And when you are eleven, the total population
of Red River will be almost 12,000, of whom
1,565 are white,
5,757 French-speaking "mixed blood" and
4,083 English-speaking "mixed blood."

At sixteen, you are married out to Quebecois settler Antoine
Couture, many years your senior. To avoid spending two days
in a Red River cart to reach the Roman Catholic church
in Winnipeg, the two of you are wed in the stone church
at St. Peter's. Your nephew claims George Kennedy officiated.

No status for you now, except that of wife.

Years later, in 1881, you tell the census man you are
Scotch, your religion Church of England. You are listed
"assistant cook," and Antoine, "cook" at St. Andrews.

Your first child, Theodore, is born in 1883 in Fort Alexander
Reserve. You call yourself Suzan in official records. You are
twenty-four. Why were you in Fort Alexander? Why no children
before this?

You caught up, however, becoming a baby-maker of eleven.
The summer you are forty-nine, you climb aboard the SS *Premier* on
a hot August day, headed for Warren's Landing.

Patient Wife

Two years after you are married, Catherine, your husband,
Antoine Couture, applies for a *licence d'auberge* in Winnipeg, although
he's a resident of Selkirk. Less than a year later, the newspaper reports:

The partnership between Antoine and Joseph Couture
as hotelkeepers at Selkirk, County of Lisgar, under the
name and style of A. and J. Couture, has this day been
dissolved by mutual consent, Antoine Couture hereby agreeing
to pay all debts contracted in the name of said firm and being
authorized to collect all debts due said firm.
Antoine Couture / Joseph Couture
Witness – Smith Vaughan

In debt now, he must have wandered around trying to find money,
because on August 9, 1879, the rascal makes the news again:

A short time ago Antoine Couture, of Selkirk, was tried before Mr. Sifton,
J. P., for selling liquor to Indians, and also for selling on Sunday, and
without license. He was found guilty, and fined $50 and costs – the latter
amounting to $17.60 – and thirty days in jail. In default of payment of the
fine he was to endure four months in durance vile. He didn't pay the fine,
neither did he go to jail, though why he didn't do one or the other one of
these things what no feller can find out. He made himself scarce, but

yesterday afternoon was captured at St. Boniface station by constables Bell and Joyal, and brought over to the city. An effort will be made to induce him to put in his four months, as requested. The usual seven-shooter and a considerable sum of money were found on him.

Upright: Or, Intelligence Comes to Red River

Testamentum from R. G. MacBeth, whose book *The Romance of Western Canada* is triumphal, as are the words of the poet MacBeth admires, John Greenleaf Whittier:

> I hear the tread of pioneers
> Of nations yet to be;
> The first low wash of waves, where soon
> Shall roll a human sea.

We are now nearing the era
of Confederation, for the provinces
in the east were getting together,

and great statesmen in those regions
were looking westward, beyond the
old horizon limits, to the wide land

stretching toward the setting sun.
The Red River folk had kept that land
British, had demonstrated

the immense possibilities of
the country and had stamped
upon the immense territory
              the seal
of upright, law-abiding,
              intelligent character.

The Girl Who Loved You So True

July 1870:

Her Majesty's Government having determined upon stationing some troops amongst you, I have been instructed by the Lieutenant-General Commanding in British North America to proceed to Fort Garry with the force under my command. Our mission is one of peace, and the sole object of the expedition is to secure Her Majesty's sovereign authority.

Come and sit by my side if you love me.

Courts of Law, such as are common to every portion of Her Majesty's Empire, will be duly established and justice will be impartially administered to all races and to all classes. The Loyal Indians of Half-breeds being as dear to our Queen as any others of Her Loyal Subjects.

Come and sit by my side.

The strictest order and discipline will be maintained and in private property will be carefully respected. All supplies furnished by the Inhabitants will be duly paid, should anyone consider himself injured by any individual attached to the force, his grievance shall be promptly enquired into.

Do not hasten to bid me adieu.

All loyal people are earnestly invited to aid me in carrying out the above-mentioned objects.

G. J. Wolseley
Colonel Commanding Red River Force

But remember the Red River Valley, and the girl
who has loved you so true.

Louis Riel, Manitoba Free Press, *February 28, 1874*

...after having thus taken possession of Fort Garry, which we had left
free to the representatives of Her Majesty, Wolseley, in a public speech,
congratulated himself and his troops at having put to flight Riel's
bandits. Such was the expression he made use of to describe the
President of the Provisional Government and his supporters.

For this long, long time I have waited
for the words that you never would say.
But now my last hope has vanished
when they tell me you're going away.

Some days later the Canadian Lieutenant Governor arrived. But he
assumed the reins of Government of our country only to consummate
the conspicuous act of perfidy of which Canada had made us
the victims. He installed himself without fulfilling the condition sine qua
non of amnesty. Thus the Canadian Government
broke from the beginning the solemn treaty
it had made with the Provisional Government.

Following the River

When you go to your home by the ocean,
may you never forget the sweet hours
that we spent in the Red River Valley
or the vows we exchanged 'mid the bowers.

Moreover, the Canadian Government had made us amicable propositions,
and when we had accepted its amnesty,
it laughed at us.

It has laughed at the public assurances, formal and spontaneous,
of amnesty given to us in January 1870, through the mouth
of Mr. D. A. Smith, now superintendent of the Hudson's Bay Company
in Manitoba and the North-West.

It has laughed at its word of honor
given us spontaneously in favour of an amnesty in May 1870,
by the mouth of His Grace, the devout Archbishop of St. Boniface.

The Canadian Confederation is, therefore,
as regards Manitoba and the North-West,
a deceit.

Will you think of the valley you're leaving?
Oh, how lonely and dreary 'twill be!
Will you think of the fond heart you're breaking
and be true to your promise to me.

This state of things has lasted three years and a half.
But the former inhabitants of Rupert's Land
and the North West have never ceased to demand what is due to them,
and which the Canadian Government owes them
under so many titles. And today more than ever,

they demand it peremptorily. What we demand is amnesty;
that is, the loyal execution of the Manitoba Act.
Nothing more, but also nothing less.

(signed) Louis Riel

Do not hasten
do not hasten to bid me adieu.

The dark maiden's prayer for her lover
to the spirit that rules o'er the world:
his pathway with sunshine may cover,
leave his grief to the Red River girl.

There could never be such a longing
in the heart of a white maiden's breast
as dwells in the heart you are breaking
with love for the boy who came west.

Come and sit by my side.

Invisible

"Indian Camp at St. Peter's [*sic*] Dynevor, Treaty Time, 1880."
Source: Robert Bell / Library and Archives Canada / PA-039918.

Enfranchise

verb [with obj.]: give the right to vote; (historical) free (a slave)

Enfranchisement, 1857–1885

noun: *"often nonconsensual process through which federal recognition of Indians was withdrawn… a concrete way to assimilate Indigenous peoples out of legislative existence, extinguish their rights, and solidify colonial control over lands and resources."* – Chelsea Vowel (âpihtawikosisân), *Indigenous Writes*

Catherine, what did your parents – an Indian and a half-breed under laws they didn't make – think about the new order? Before you were born, folks out east passed the *Act to Encourage the Gradual Civilization of Indian Tribes in this Province, and to Amend the Laws Respecting Indians.*

Your lot must be civilized. And, through the process of enfranchisement, any legal distinctions between Indians and non-Indians can, in time, be erased. You can be absorbed into the Canadian body politic.

In 1867, Queen Victoria says yes to the *British North America Act*, and the "new" country your ancestors lived in for thirty thousand years is to be called Canada. O Canada.

Following the River

In 1870, Manitoba becomes "the postage stamp province."
In 1871, your father is present at the signing of Treaty 1.
In 1876, Indians become wards of the state.
In 1876, Edith MacTavish, daughter of the chief factor at
Norway House, is born. In 1920, she will become the first woman
of Métis ancestry to be elected to the Manitoba legislature.

In 1876, you marry out. No status for you.

(And sorry, no voting in Canadian elections either. According to
Section 86[1] of the *Indian Act*, only a male Indian over twenty-one
with a university degree can be enfranchised in the eyes of this new
Canada.)

Do Sally and Antoine talk at church, on Treaty Day, at gatherings, do –
or can – they read, attend town hall meetings, have a sense what
this new federation will bring? Red River is home – all its abundance
and scarcity, its harsh cold and hot, insect-ravaged summers. Perhaps
for your parents, home is you and your siblings, their buried infants,
grandchildren who will live on into the years ahead, scattered in the
prairie wind. Their property – cows, crops – numbered and divided,
reduced to pen and ink. What does country mean?

In 1883, Antoine Kennedy, your father, dies. Your mother, Sally,
takes scrip. A complicated transaction with a simple goal: cash for
your right to call yourself Métis. What did Sally do with $80, $160,
$240 Canadian – a month's worth of groceries today, or a laptop if
you can find a deal? (Three years later, Catherine, you will apply for
scrip, as will, in the rules of the day, your Quebecois husband.)

In 1885, Sir John A. is about to extend the vote to all Indians but:
the resistance.

And Indigenous women? They watch through windows as the rights of their white sisters are debated.

~

Franchise, 1886
noun: the right to vote in political elections. Also: suffrage.

Brandon Sun Weekly, March 25, 1886.
Shall the franchise be extended to (white) women?

At the meeting of the Junior Liberal Association of this city held on Thursday evening, March 18, in the Masonic Hall, the debate was opened by Mr. Young, who said:

"Progress in many lives was slow and will be so until many changes are made. Woman is the better Christian of mankind, therefore when she goes to the poll her vote is likely to be a more sensible one, as shown in the late Toronto municipal election.... The wrong man wears the trousers. For many years she has studied medicine and law and has outstripped in numerous instances her male competitors. Can we therefore say she has not as good brain power as man?"

Mr. Terryberry said:
"History gives us no instance whatever to justify such a step, neither profane nor biblical. It would be a discredit to man to acknowledge, by such an extension of the franchise, that he was not equal to such duties which are his alone. If such an extension be made then we must have them as judges, lawyers, senators and everything which is man's work and most decidedly not hers. They have enough to do in the home life without dabbling in politics."

W. H. Irwin next took up the debate, asking:
"What had woman ever done to be deprived of the privilege to vote? There is no liberty of speech as far as the ladies are concerned, nor does it show fair play to keep them back in any way. Their moral character is generally better than man's. A dishonest man, a man most immoral in character, is often brought to the front. Men, full of all the vileness of which man is capable, may be lauded and praised while women of a far superior moral character must be excluded from using her influence for good to the fullest extent. Why should she not have a voice in the nation's affairs, while man who is a long way behind her in true goodness should be to the front?"

Mr. Robert Matheson then followed by remarking:
"...it was claimed that the woman's vote turned the Toronto election, which was scarcely correct, for the majority was sufficient without their vote. It would scarcely seem a fit and proper thing to see them on a driz-zling day busying themselves with such matters as they did in Toronto. They are capable of busying themselves in very questionable ways as shown by their action in Birmingham, England, when they tried to effect a change in its representation by working in the way of canvassing against the Right Honourable John Bright. God has many spheres for women to work in, and also other spheres for men, and this power of voting is man's, and ought not to be woman's in a universal sense, exemplifying the maxum 'the hand that rock's the cradle rocks the nation.'

After further general discussion, it was decided to again introduce the subject at some future meeting.

The next meeting will be held in the same place on April 1, when a debate will take place on the subject:

Resolved the government were justified in the imprisonment of Half Breeds and Indians after the late rebellion.

∽

Enfranchise, 1959–1985

West and south of the city, cold hands haul water during bitter Winnipeg winters to the rough shacks of scrap boxcar lumber and metal. Homes of no fixed address, no plumbing. In the spring of 1959, with Mayor Juba at the helm, the city gives Métis families $50 – some say $75 – so developers can build a high school and then a mall. The families are moved into social housing in the north end. Now they can vote. In Selkirk, Catherine, your adult children, if they own property, can cast a ballot.

In 1971, a charismatic man with a rose in his lapel marries a young white girl. Helen Betty Osborne moves in with a Caucasian family in The Pas, Manitoba, and now, off reserve, is eligible to vote. Meanwhile, east of the Prairies, Mary Two-Axe Earley has been writing letters to the government about the price of enfranchisement. The price of being a woman. It is not until 1985 she'll gain back her status. Her hands were verbs.

∽

Following the River

Enfranchise
origin: franc, franche (free)

liberty
to free from a burden
to free from a restriction
a special privilege granted to a person or a group
a constitutional or statutory right or privilege
the right to vote
to free from slavery
the right of suffrage
to admit to political privileges
to allow
to allow is

transitive
transitive
transitive

from *transitivus* – to go across

A bridge, a crossing, a passage.

– *empower*, a benefactor word doling out
gifts and favours and license –
deigning to let her speak, let her vote on
how she will spend her day, her season, her life,
whether she can be free from blows, pain, humiliation,
fear, loneliness, misery, mule work, shame, obscurity
and take up the joys of making, creating, learning,
to breathe whole, move freely, go from being told
to telling, away from the fathers of her world –

missionaries, permission-aries, officialdom, rules,
where no syntax of blood and bone can render her passive,
stuck in a sentence that buries her birthright, stakes
a claim to her body,
silences.

Entitled to begin every day with *I*.

Town Kisser

A note about Selkirk resident Mrs. Johnson in 1882.

Noted characters around the town were Geordie Boy,
a half-breed who could imitate a donkey braying and
a Mrs. Johnson, a French half-breed who lived to be 121,
bore twenty-three children, and every New Year's it was her
custom to kiss every man in town, expecting ten cents, which
she spent on firewater.

Where They Cannot Find Her: May 12, 1885

Josephte Desjarlais Delorme (1863–1936)

Red uniforms rush down the hill, bullets fly
around her, so Josephte places her baby, Sarah,
in a washtub. "Run away," William tells his wife,
and she hurries past strewn bodies, reaches
the river, where hard rain hammers on the surface:
soldiers' bullets.

Resisters have hung their coats and caps on
low-hanging branches, and Middleton's men will
    fight the clothes all day.

"We kill many soldiers that day," she says, "but we
lose thirteen Indians and three half-breeds, and everything

we have: about thirty-five horses, and all the wagons."

And Josephte's little black mare, Jessy,
who once was wild, breaks her rope and runs
into the bushes, where the white men
cannot find her.

Doing Laundry in the Resistance

Eleanore Thomas Garneau (1852–1912)

Eleanore Garneau is in the kitchen doing laundry the day
the North West Mounted Police ride up with a search warrant.

Louis Riel has returned north, stirring excitement in the region.
Eleanore and Lawrence have moved west from Red River to

stake a claim along the Saskatchewan, and Eleanore, a calm,
hard-working woman fluent in both Gaelic and Cree, remains

silent as she watches a sergeant arrest her husband while four
constables stride through the house, looking in vain for a letter

Riel had sent to Lawrence about support for the resistance, a letter
he would read to men who could not. Eleanore scrubs, rubbing

shirts over the ribs of the washboard until what she'd tucked inside
their folds turns to soggy bits, ink leaching into the cooling water.

Sister Annie Goulet

b. 1842 – d. 1917

At three, Annie Goulet brings candy to the baby Jesus
in the crèche at church. A child smitten with a child.
At twenty-one, Annie offers herself to the Lord, but
                    the order isn't sure it will have her.

Les Soeurs Grises had come to Red River in 1844 from Montreal.
Fifty-nine days in a canoe, fighting off mosquitoes, soaking up
the damp and cold in clothing unsuitable for travel, surviving
on few provisions. Their first house an oven in summer, an
icebox in winter. Later, in their own, larger building, they
feed seventeen wood stoves.

Then comes pestilence – measles, dysentery, famine. In 1852,
the flood. From the top floor of their building, the nuns watch
flood waters rise, destroy crops, wash away herds of animals.
Still, they prevail.
                    Medicine: plantain, goldenrod,
cherry tree bark. Washing and more washing. Tending to
sorry souls, heathens, the wretched.

One sister, Sainte-Thérèse, on loan from Montreal, is called
back east in 1859, but on the way, Louis Riel Senior

Following the River

and a group of Métis intercept, kidnapping their beloved
Soeur Docteur and sending her back in a Red River cart
to where she is most wanted.

But Annie Goulet, the child who loves the baby Jesus –

Annie is Métis. Bishop Taché wants God's word to spread
in Red River, at least among girls, and he knows young
Métis men do not want to be taught by women.

        Taché knows colony postulants as

"charming children whose knowledge of Indian languages
will allow them to render us essential services in the future."

Such a postulant is Annie Goulet, loved by the children
because she speaks to them in Cree and Saulteaux.

        (The first of the young
"Métisses" out West to join had been Marguerite Connolly,
daughter of fur trader William Connolly, and great-niece
of the founder of the order. After William had turned off
his country wife, Miyo Nipiy [Suzanne Pas-de-Nom], in Norway
House, she brought her daughter Marguerite to Red River,
where Marguerite joined the order in 1845.)

After all, the Grey Nuns claim all sisters, whether "blond,
dark or brunette," are one.

Mostly.

It depends.

In 1862, Annie Goulet is ready to give herself to the Lord.
A thousand miles away, in Montreal, Superior-General
Sister Slocombe stalls: Is Annie's kind
strong enough,
dedicated enough?

> *Métis, especially the women,*
> *are fickle.*

Haven't the other sisters in Red River
expressed concern about their perseverance?

And so, Annie and a young Salish woman, Mary-Jane McDougall,
are made to wait.

And wait.

No approval comes.

Bishop Taché plunges ahead, holds a public ceremony,
admitting the half-breed novices. Soon another Métis joins
the fold – Sara Riel, sister of Louis.

Sara and Annie, each with notable brothers. As Red River hostilities
grow, Sara writes Louis: "We must find in religion

the balm of our sorrow." Annie's brother, Elzéar Goulet,
a mail carrier, joins Riel's men.

Les Soeurs are sympathetic to the cause, and
Annie and Sara pray for their brothers.

Following the River

March 1870: Métis guards kill Thomas Scott, who becomes
a martyr for the anti-Catholic, the anti-French.

Elzéar Goulet is among those held responsible.
In September, two of Wolseley's men
stone Elzéar to death as he tries to swim
across the river to St. Boniface.

Louis flees to the United States.

Elzéar's body washes up on the banks, and Annie
learns his seventeen-year-old daughter, Laurette, was
raped by members of the Red River Expeditionary
Force, and has died. The colonel in charge, told of
RREF's attacks on women, says: "What my soldiers do
is none of my business."

> (One of the RREF is Louis Couture,
> a pro-Canadian settler who wants
> to quash the Métis, later praised on his
> death as a distinguished pioneer.)

> (His leader, Wolseley, a four-continent
> fighter, becomes a viscount, and now
> sits in bronze on a steed in Horse Guards
> Parade in London.)

Years later, Annie Goulet moves farther west to an industrial
school at Lebret, not yet Saskatchewan, where she serves her
beloved Lord Jesus until 1917. The school, opened in 1884, sits
overlooking the river in the Qu'Appelle Valley.

196

I think of Annie now, her grief on losing her brother,
her steady friendship with Sara,
and I wonder, as she prays her last prayer,

does she recall the baby in the crèche,
the voices of young Cree by the Red,
that day in November 1870 when she
and Sara are asked to greet the new
lieutenant governor, a man

emboldened with fresh victory?

How the man strides into the school, taking
particular notice of Annie and Sara, nods
with a thin smile at the sight
of the welcome sign above the door?

The Indian Question: What Settler Women Say

1886 Survey

Do you experience any dread of the Indians?

No, they are perfectly quiet and harmless.

I've not seen an Indian for months.

None whatever; I have visited them here in their tents.

I have had, but not now.

Poor things, no. I often like to feed them when they come around.

I hope the different churches will soon have them Christianized.

No, not any, and I live close near an Indian reserve.

Have only seen two in the last five years.

The Indians call in but are very friendly.

Not the least; in fact, in point of honour in any dealings we have with them, they put some of the whites to shame.

I have never seen any since I came to the farm, now going on three years.

Never think of them.

None whatever, although they often call at my house to sell fish and wild fruit.

No, no, no. I had a fear of them before coming here, but have found those on our reserve a quite inoffensive lot, and have had them working on the farm several times. They are Presbyterians.

I was in dread of them last spring, but I don't mind them now, as the disturbance is all over with them.

No; nor did we ever during the rebellion.
No, I rather like them.
No, the squaws will wash and scrub for you.
None whatever. They are all right if treated kindly but firmly.
The Indians are all right if people would let them alone.
They are kind and civil.
The government will see after the Indians in the future.
Not very much; only I do not like them.

Not now; for some years I felt uncomfortable at receiving visits from them, but now often find them most useful "helps."

Not any. My husband is an Indian agent.
I sometimes accompany him to the reserves, where there are a number of them.

No; no more dread than I would have in Toronto.

No fear of the red man.

Not in the least, never did. We employ them continually, and treat them honestly, and they fear and respect us.

I hire a squaw to do my scrubbing.
I often wish they would come 'round with mats and baskets.

Don't Spoil Your Looks

Brandon Daily Sun, December 22, 1904

It should be the aim of every woman
to master the expression of her face.
Expression is the action of certain
muscles of the face. Joy, sadness, love,
hate, fear or anger, each calls into play
a set of muscles. The habitual use of one
of these leaves on the countenance marks
which tell their own story, says the
Montreal Herald. Cultivate placidity
of expression, and rest assured that there
will be no danger of vacancy of countenance.
Avoid wrinkling your brow, closing one
eye, frowning, sniffling, "turning up the
nose," thrusting the tongue into the
cheek, pouting, pointing the lips, pursing
up the mouth or letting it loll open,
opening widely the eyes, wagging the head,
grinning, or otherwise twisting or
contorting the feathers. It means sure
damage to a pretty face and is inconsistent
with good breeding.

All the Names

Testamentum from Rev. R. G. MacBeth, clergyman and historian:

*The practice of naming the child "after" someone was much in
vogue, and led sometimes to dilemmas and difficulties. For instance,
when two or more near relatives on either side were to be considered,
the parents were in serious straits lest they should give offence to
the one or the other. The difficulty had to be faced, and the danger
braved, or else the child had to be encumbered with a string
of names such as only foreign princes can boast, and we have
even known an irate friend or relative mollified by the promise,
that on a similar occasion in the future he or she should not
be overlooked.*

*Another of the difficulties resulting from the now (fortunately)
almost obsolete custom of "naming" was not only the duplicating
but the quadruplicating of names in the one neighborhood.
The people got over that part of the trouble by introducing the use
of "nick-names," derived either from personal characteristics or by
prefixing or affixing some ancestral family name. This was well
enough for the people themselves who knew locally "Black Sandy"
and "Red Sandy," but since people at a distance did not know these
fine shades of distinction, the primitive post office or the mail-carrier
confronted "confusion worse confounded" when a letter came addressed to*

a name owned by half a dozen different people in the parish. The difficulty
was generally solved by some one of the name opening it, and
if it was not for him he passed it on till the right party was reached.

Once Upon a Bird

ocicahk (crane)

*The sandhill crane was easy to approach, especially between
the end of August and mid-September, because it was so
curious. It would rush to investigate as soon as it saw
anything unusual. With a wing span of four or five feet,
it could weigh as much as twelve pounds. The meat was
excellent, a lot like turkey.*

cahcahkâyow (blackbird)

*...and we also ate owl, and blackbirds. I remember the blackbirds;
my mom used to entrap them, she had made the trap for herself
by nailing boards together; she propped it up with little sticks and when
the blackbirds came to eat underneath the board, she jerked out
the little sticks and brought the board down on the blackbirds,
and then she made soup for us...*

pipiciw, âkiskow (robin, partridge)

Bird Jelly for Convalescents:

*Put twelve fat, well prepared robins, or six partridges in
a saucepan with one quart of water; cover closely,*

*and set on the fire. Boil gently until the birds are ready to pull
to pieces, and the water is reduced to half a pint. Strain through
a colander and piece of muslin and skim off the grease
carefully. Salt to taste and pour into four
little fancy moulds.*

This is very delicate and nutritious.

kihci niska, or **niski mîcimâpowiy** (Canada goose)

Goose Soup
Recipe by Mary M'Lot, Cross Lake
- *1 Canada goose, cut into parts*
- *2 cups navy beans or another type (rinsed)*
- *1 onion, diced vegetables – whatever you have (carrots, celery, roots, turnip, squash, etc.)*
- *salt and pepper to taste*
- *serve with bannock*

*It really affects everybody, it affects everything, the hydro project. Even
the birds that fly around, the geese and the ducks and everything. Because
they have to feed on grass, on little insects, whatever they eat, and they
get affected by mercury. It's not only fish that are affected by mercury, it's
also the flying creatures. Now they say you can't eat the liver of a moose;
pretty soon they're going to say you cannot eat the geese or the ducks.*
– Grand Council of the Crees

Klondike Kitty: Sarah Ann Catherine Couture

b. 1880 – d. 1915

Klondike Kitty

Dawson Record, September 15, 1903

> *Miss Katherine Couture has been paying farewell visits this*
> *week to her many friends on Last Chance Creek. Miss Couture's*
> *parents were pioneers in the northwest and reside at present*
> *near Selkirk, Manitoba, to where she goes direct from here. Miss*
> *Couture's brothers and sisters always speak of her in her absence*
> *as Klondike Kitty. Since arriving in this country Miss Couture*
> *has run a hotel near the mouth of Hunker Creek first in company*
> *with her father and later with her brother Alfred, and her excel-*
> *lent deportment and bright, cheerful ways have won her hosts of*
> *friends in the Klondike. Her Last Chance friends gave a party in*
> *her honor at the Bachelors' Hall Saturday evening which was an*
> *enjoyable affair. Miss Couture will leave Dawson in a day or two*
> *and will be greatly missed.*

All your names. Catherine, Katherine, Katie, Catie, Sarah Ann and
Kate.

And now Kitty. Klondike Kitty. Miss Couture.

Following the River

Parents were pioneers? A little story goes a long way when you're thousands of kilometres away from Red River.

Look at you in this photograph. Starched white shirt, a tie with a pin, your dark hair pulled back. Distinctive lips, sharp eyes.

In 1896, the northwest erupted with the discovery of gold. Thousands rushed to the Klondike from the US and Canada, including your uncles Louis and Philip Couture; your father, Antoine; your brother Alfred. You were young; sixteen or so, if census records are accurate.

Those men first stepped off the ship in San Francisco with stories of rich ore, a bonanza, free for the taking, and the world was abuzz. Did the men want a housekeeper? Did you want freedom? Your mother's last child was an infant when you left, a child whose birth records I can't find. Did your mother simply say, "Go, child, I've got this?"

Last Chance Creek and a roadhouse near Hunker Creek. Nearby, the Bonanza Stables run by Alfred and later, by the hulking Australian you would marry. The worldwide stampede made Dawson City the fastest-growing town in North America at the time.

Catie/Kitty, you return to Selkirk in 1903. By then, the gold rush is over. Many leave the Klondike at the turn of the century, when Nome, Alaska, becomes the draw.

But how long you stay "outside" is a mystery. A few years later, you return north to Hunker Creek, where you work in the roadhouse owned by your uncle Louis. You meet Norman Nicholas Graeber (Graber), an Australian adventurer who has travelled across the globe to look for gold. In the only photograph I have, you and your friend stand behind a fierce-looking man the size of a silverback gorilla.

You bear the man's child, Anthony Gerald Graeber, born June 23, 1907.

Was baby Anthony your parents' first grandchild? Anthony: likely named for your father or grandfather, both Antoine. The delivery is difficult, and the baby is sickly.

The story goes that Graeber leaves the infant out in the woodpile to die. The baby is a month old: July 26, 1907. A lummox, this man. And – I wonder if you knew – a bigamist who left a wife and several children in Australia.

Dawson Record, April 3, 1908

Pioneer Dies: Had Appendicitis
Suffered from complaint for some time – wife now outside

Norman Nicholas Graeber, proprietor of the Bonanza stables, on Turner Street, died at 3 o'clock this morning at the Good Samaritan Hospital of the results of appendicitis. He was operated on yesterday afternoon.

Mr. Graeber had been ill with appendicitis a few weeks ago and recovered so that he was able to leave his bed and get about at his work again. A few days ago he was taken ill a second time, and a day or two ago had to go to the hospital.

The deceased came here from Seattle. He originally was from Australia. He was a man of large and apparently rugged physique. For two or three years he had been proprietor of the Bonanza stables. Two years ago he was married in Dawson. His wife left last fall for the outside for a visit, and is still there.

Her brother is in the city and will arrange for the funeral.

Mrs. Graeber nearly lost her life last summer following the arrival of their first child, which died. The mother was in bed many weeks.

Your husband dies in the spring of 1908. Did you leave for a visit, or to work with your father at Warren's Landing? Were you one of the daughters near the wharf when your mother died later that year?

By this time, your uncle Louis's roadhouse, like so many stables, roadhouses and storefronts, has gone out of business, and the area –

with its untravelled roads, abandoned mines and empty buildings – is filled with silence. Some say there is still a "Couture's Bend" in the area. Others say gold was found under your uncle Louis's roadhouse when it was torn down.

No way to tell. You leave Canada for the Seattle area, where Alfred and other Couture relatives are living, and die March 23, 1915, at the age of thirty-five, a month before Aunt Kay, your niece, is born.

You are buried in Woodinville, Washington.

I hope someone stood at your grave.

Klondike Kitty: Sarah Ann Catherine (Kitty) Couture. Photo courtesy of Robert Couture.

"I am on way home"

Catherine, was your son an adventurer? In Winnipeg, my cousin Ray hands me a tattered dark green postcard – one of the earliest of its kind – sent from Seattle, Washington, to you. We think it's date-stamped 1905. A two-page, single-fold, thick paper, oiled or waxed. Inside, a panoramic view of the city. Is this the closest you came to adventure?

July 1897: a steamship from Alaska arrives in the Seattle port, bearing prospectors and gold, and the rush from Seattle begins. Did Napoleon decide not to go? Was he visiting an uncle? Fourteen years later, Louis Napoleon marries Marie Antoinette Poirier. You have died by then.

I hold the postcard; your fingerprints may still be on it. The connection is a shock. When you opened the fold, Catherine, you would have seen your son's tiny script below the coloured cityscape: *I am on way home.*

Catherine Kennedy Couture's daughters. Photo courtesy of Katherine (Kay) Reynaud.

This Moon

– on a Nova Scotia shore

The last time the moon was this close to the earth
I was fresh from my mother's womb. This night,
memories of summer – its salt taste, its calming
hush of waves at the edge of the Atlantic – are still
within reach. The old road to the shore is banked with
trees, my feet unsteady on ruts and gravel, and when
I come into the open, her light is on me before her
low-slung silhouette appears.

A rumble, a quaking in the bush –
hooves – and four or five shapes fly past the moon's
bright face, disappear into the trees. She is steady,
this moon, and tonight ample, solid, tugging
water and blood as if to gather us in her skirts,
wrap us in their sway.
                    Praise this moon;
her generous, brimming light reaches deep into waters
to lift them toward the stars, let them down again.
Even in the longest day, when it seems she has disappeared,
she waits, glistening on rocky shoals, other riverbanks,
the wings of birds and eyes of animals
who find solace in the dark. I am

Following the River

one of them, an animal watching the moon's brush
paint the bay, imagining her light on the faces of mothers
I never knew but whose bodies carried a fleck
of who I might become. Who many of us are. All
those who rose from the land, knew it more deeply
than we can ever know. Lived on the brink of water
and hope, bore children ripped from them,
believed men they should not have, built a hearth
to burn long after their names and bodies were gone.
Above me, the sky is silver-stitched, the stars a past
we reach for in the present, and all the while the moon
gazes, placid, radiant, her elegant fingers touching us all.

Crows have settled for the night, deer have found refuge
from human footfall, and I walk bearing the gifts of those
before me, unsure I deserve them. I am the result, the poet says,
of the love of thousands; yet I carry, too, the ways they
were lost, found, torn from the world, abused, scorned yet
defiant, persistent, spirited, strong, gilded with the lustre
only the moon can deliver.

Riverbank, marsh, bog, bush and plain, rough water, knee-deep
mud and clouds of dust, swarms and famine, disease, back-
scorching heat. Ribbons of sweat on their breasts, blood of
afterbirth between their legs. Burdens I cannot imagine.

I return to the house with the moon rising in the south,
shaken by all I am given. This much I know:
I must split open, scatter my life like moonlight –
nîpâyâstew – across everything I thought I knew, seek out
dark roads, underbellies of leaves and old creeds, crack

silence, learn how the breath of the dead inspires the living,
submit to neap, spring, ebb, flood, again and again. Make
each morning a prayer to whisper in the ear of time.

Part Three: The Road Back

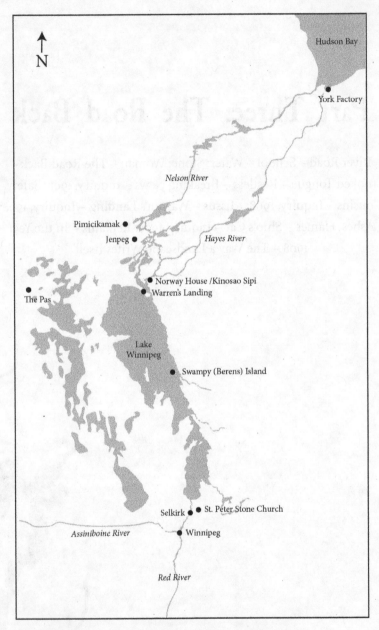

Map of Red River to Norway House courtesy of Kathy Kaulbach,
Touchstone Design House.

River Road

The first of May, a Sunday, and I turn the car north to The Pas, where I will be working for six weeks as writer-in-residence. It's the beginning of a pilgrimage of sorts, but I don't know this now.

I veer off the main highway and take River Road. I want to stop again at the water's edge in Selkirk, where Catherine might have boarded the SS *Premier* and set sail north on Lake Winnipeg. My greatest hope – and I fear hoping too much will jinx the possibility – is to find my way eventually from The Pas to Norway House, and then out on the water to Warren's Landing, where the SS *Premier*'s voyage ended. I need to see where Catherine died, to walk that shore.

It's been a year of immersing myself in the stories of women, trying to imagine the lives of my grandmothers and other Red River women. The back-breaking work, bearing and losing babies, crop infestations, diseases, violence, class struggles, poverty – as a descendant freed from some of these circumstances, I owe it to the women of my past to acknowledge the stamina, spirit and strength they needed merely to survive. The majority of "half-breed" women didn't have the relatively privileged lives of the Prudens, Bannatynes, Ballendens or Sinclairs, yet all suffered under the weight of political tensions and racial hostilities, their voices muted, their bodies tethered to domestic concerns. Their white (or white-leaning) sisters were silenced, too, but they had the benefit of a staunch belief in their own superiority and plenty of evidence of its social benefits. The poet Linda Hogan claims I am the result of "the love of thousands." More likely, I am the result of tenacity and endurance beyond my capacity to understand.

The past is not far away, however. It reveals itself in newspaper headlines, in the need for an inquiry into the deaths and disappearance of countless Indigenous women and girls. It's here in the box of books beside me, in raw and vivid accounts of contemporary women such as Maria Campbell, a Métis woman from Alberta, whose young womanhood exemplifies what our nation's colonial mindset has produced.

It's here in the shadowy past of this old road, River Road. This route, now cultivated and manicured, paved and divided into private properties, would likely have been the route Antoine and Sally Kennedy travelled, and likely in a Red River cart or on foot.

As I follow the shore of the Red, I am entering the landscape that bore them, driving over old footprints long disappeared under snows and rains and the press of "progress."

Beside me, I have a map of the area, apparently drawn by Reverend Cowley, the man who succeeded Cockran in 1858, the same year Catherine Kennedy was born. "Grand Rapids," it reads – that would likely mean where the Lockport dam is now. Water Mill, Whirlpool Point and the Big Eddy, Indian School and Sugar Point. He has marked Elm and Aspens, Small Aspen, Oak, Elm and Maple.

Indian Village. Black ink, smudged, crude marks to indicate trees, lines to separate the end of St. Andrews Parish and the beginning of St. Peter's, just before Sugar Point, or what is now the waterfront area of Selkirk.

"Never flooded." The words at the top of the drawing mark the west side of the river above the old stone fort, Lower Fort Garry. Ah yes, floods. Since 1826, the Red has flooded more than twenty times, often with great devastation.

In Catherine's lifetime, there were two major floods, one in 1861 and one in 1882. The *Church Guardian* newspaper headline in 1882 read:

"A Modern Venice Without Its Beauty." Furniture floated in houses, and the river rose eight metres above its normal height. Winter snow and ice jams were thought to be the cause, and the Canadian Pacific Railway immediately took measures to protect its line in the future. The following winter, Catherine gave birth to her son Theodore in Fort Alexander; did she travel north because of the flood? In Manitoba, everyone has a flood story. In 1950, my husband's family moved in with his grandparents – fish swam in Winnipeg streets.

When I reach the first tourist information stop on River Road, flies buzz in the spring sun and birds are busy. As I stand on the banks of the Red, the erosion below makes me think about what the river has taken over the last century.

Behind me are large permanent displays, or "interpretive nodes," as they are called. I tend always to read educational display boards, even as I understand the information has been reduced to its most basic. And here, the display uses a common trope: to imagine a family of the time and tell the story through them. Here, I see young Annie is the stand-in for Everygirl.

Pock: a distinctive sound. Across the road, a Sunday morning group of men with their caddies, dressed in smart chinos and short-sleeved shirts. Golf is generally credited to the Scots. I can't even imagine what the Scots who farmed along this river would make of this well-heeled crew.

At the next stop, the interpretive display board is titled "Clap and Squeal" and it reads:

Curse the south wind if you were rowing to Fort Garry. At Fort Garry you unloaded the goods from London, then loaded the furs and started rowing back to York Factory. You are a smart girl, Annie. Can you guess where the boats got their name?

A whiff of weed is coming from the park bench nearby – a couple watching the geese – but I'm trying to decipher the text on the board.

Following the River

Do we know if Annie is one of the Scottish or English settlers or from an Indigenous family? We know the York boats travelled north on this river for decades, workhorses loaded down with goods headed for York Factory and back again, propelled by the massive efforts of Native men, tripmen, some of whom, I have since learned, were Kennedys.

Clap and squeal? Annie, dear – I do hope you can figure out where the boats got their name.

I feel the sting of annoyance at all this. I appreciate these interpretive nodes are helpful for tourists and school tours, but I wonder what good comes from such radical simplification of history. Is this information better than nothing at all? Perhaps I am too immersed in Red River history these days, filled with chagrin about my own ignorance and lack of curiosity, challenged by the enormity of a shared past few have acknowledged. After all, if I'd driven along River Road years ago, I, too, might have taken these signs for what they were – history lite – and not given it a thought.

As if to punctuate my irritation, I notice a tick on my arm when I reach for my keys, and just then, three motorcycles roar past, spitting gravel at my leg as I open the car door.

What do we owe the past? My mother would regale us with stories of her grandfather Carson Glenn, one of the early settlers in the Strathclair, Manitoba, area. He was Scottish, as was his bride, and the Glenn brothers had a hand in constructing many town buildings. They arrived in the late 1800s, farmed, raised children, had their own family dramas and betrayals. After our mother died, my sister and brother and I went to the town's 150-year celebration and met several Glenns still living in the area. My brother, our second cousin and I spent the next day in the railway-station-turned-museum looking for Glenn traces, trying to imagine our relatives in a horse and sleigh, in hockey gear, at a washtub, standing over a hot summer stove putting up what they'd grown that year, labelling it for the annual fair.

Had my sister and brother and I lived in a community with a dozen or more cousins, I wonder if we would be as drawn to the details of our parents' and grandparents' pasts as we are. My husband admits he has little interest in knowing about his past. That baffles me.

A car speeds by and I realize I've been sitting at the side of the road daydreaming.

Where we come from isn't only place. And it isn't only people. Our foundation is not ashes or DNA, not cemetery stones, our father's temper or our grandmother's eyes.

It's a bloodline. Of stories.

My next stop is the Twin Oaks site. In Red River's heyday, this was the location of the celebrated Matilda Davis's school.

When I drive up, two young women are sitting behind their car in the dirt near the bushes overlooking the river. It seems an odd – possibly dangerous – spot to sit.

The stone structure across the road, built around the time Catherine Kennedy was born, replaced an earlier building. It housed about forty girls, all of whom were daughters of Hudson's Bay Company officials or Red River families who could afford the £132 tuition for finer education. Miss Matilda Davis turned young women into English ladies. Here they were taught the womanly arts of music, dancing, deportment, etiquette and French – *un peu* at least.

Nearby, another display board describes the missionary schools begun by Reverend William Cockran and his wife, Ann. It's unclear to me whether this school was located near Miss Davis's. Meant for "mixed-blood" children, Cockran's day school "taught girls cooking, sewing and proper wifely attitudes like being obedient to one's husband."

Not the skills Miss Davis's students would learn. Kathleen McDermot Truthwaite describes her time with Miss Davis: "They used to say that after a girl came out of Miss Davis's school, she sat down as though she had a basket of eggs balanced on her head, and that you could pick out Miss Davis's pupils anywhere." She added: "When Miss

Following the River

Davis told us that the world was round like an orange and slightly flat-
tened at the poles, she had to explain to us what an orange was like, for
of course none of us had ever seen one."

Miss Davis's charges read the Scriptures regularly and walked together to St. Andrews church, about a kilometre and a half down the
road, closer to Selkirk.

I still have no idea where Catherine went to school.

I walk across the road to take a photo. This is one of well-known
stonemason Duncan McRae's structures. Now it's called Twin Oaks
and is a private residence with an address: 292 River Road. I learn later
that, at 159 years as of this writing, it's the oldest occupied home in
Canada. When it was bought in 1998, the owners gutted and restored
it, and listed it for $1.1 million. Now it belongs to former politician
Otto Lang.

Some historians have described Miss Matilda Davis's school/Twin
Oaks as the precursor to Winnipeg's private girls' school, Balmoral
Hall. I'm sure Twin Oaks would have been as distant a possibility for
Catherine as Balmoral was for me.

Behind me, a sudden loud whirring, and the two young women
who were sitting on the ground behind their car race past me on roller
skates, headed north toward St. Andrews.

I drink in the quiet for a few moments. Around me are old trees
that may have witnessed the days of early Red River, birds whose ancestors may have flown here, overgrown land and buildings inhabited
by both the quick and the dead.

Do stories linger in the air? Oh, to be able to call them down.

By the time I reach St. Andrews, the warm weather and the Western
sun have dissolved my grumpy mood. Bells are ringing as I near the
church, and people are gathered at the entrance. Of course, Sunday
service. Boys clamber over the stone wall in what looks to be their
Sunday clothes, and men in suits and smartly dressed women stand
outside holding cups of tea and plates of cake.

There it is again: that small jolt, a kind of vertigo, when I am with people in or near structures several generations older than we are. A tourist walking around the Acropolis, a child climbing a castle stair-case, a dolmen on a cliff – echoes of so many pasts.

Inside the church, the beams and short doors are intact. The ceiling is low.

I don't enter the nave, the main area, but stay inside the entrance, looking closely at the construction, trying to imagine the souls who came and went here, many of whom I'd be related to. Outside I find Reverend William Cockran's crypt a few feet from the building. Near it, children shriek in play, and around me stragglers from the congregation begin making moves to leave. The simplicity of it all reminds me of my 1950s childhood, when everything seemed straightforward. I look closely at the stained glass and remember it was likely brought upriver by a York boat.

The following year, my sister, Allison, and I will take the same route up River Road, and we'll stop at the church on our way to St. Peter's to see Wendy, the caretaker. Another spring, more gardens in bloom. I walk among the gravestones, hoping once more to find a family grave. Peter Erasmus Sr. is buried at St. Andrews, but many of the stones have fallen, faded, and even rubbing my fingers gently over the indistinct letters and dates reveals little.

As I head out on River Road again, I turn up the soft rock on the radio and take in the sights of several large, newly built houses along the way. All are designed to look older than they are, in the "historical vernacular." This is the kind of area my family would tour on a Sunday. "Let's go look at where the rich people live," my dad would say, "then go for ice cream."

I slow down near the Kennedy house, famous as the residence of Captain William Kennedy and, until recently, the site of a tea house. Another fieldstone building constructed by Duncan McRae in Gothic revival and christened by the Kennedys "Maple Grove." Kennedy was a Hudson's Bay Company employee and Arctic explorer, a half-breed celebrated as a man who helped "open up" the West. His English wife, Eleanor Cripps Kennedy, was known for her community and missionary work.

In the late 1860s, Eleanor Kennedy organized a bazaar and clothing drive for the destitute affected by a grasshopper plague. Apparently, her height, aristocratic bearing and confidence caused Reverend Canon John Grisdale to dub her a prima donna. Known more affectionately as The Duchess, Eleanor also organized community arts activities and campaigned for a hospital in the area. As her husband's health deteriorated and their finances dwindled, she took on work teaching music at Miss Davis's school and started a haberdashery business.

Sorting through my mother's files after she died, I found a brochure for the Kennedy tea house, which Mom must have visited at one time. Her notes about the captain are in the margin of the brochure: *most likely the father of Catherine Kennedy.* This, of course, is not true. William was the son of Alexander Kennedy, whose more than ten children – acknowledged and not – were all born in the first two decades of the 1800s. His son John was the first born, and William among the last. If related at all, Catherine Kennedy's father, Antoine Kennedy, might have been Alexander's bastard son, making Captain William Kennedy Antoine's half-brother. But even that's a stretch, I think.

Mom's note amused me. When I was a child, my mother had nothing but scorn for "half-breeds," but I guess if the half-breed is a famous one such as William Kennedy, you can make an exception and bask in the reflected shine. To her dying day, she was sure her own father, William Glenn, was a relative of the astronaut John Glenn. It's a human impulse, though. After all, I was surprised and delighted to be able to trace my Budd and Erasmus connections and learn about their places in this country's shared history.

William Kennedy's wife was named Eleanor. My grandmother – Catherine's daughter – was named Eleanore. Would Sally and Antoine

Kennedy and their children, including Catherine, have been among the families Eleanor Kennedy helped during those years? Am I romanticizing? Probably.

I'll need to pick up the pace to arrive at The Pas in time. Ahead, I see Lockport and the famous Skinner's, the Sunday destination of Winnipeggers for decades, the oldest hot dog stand around. Jimmy Skinner started it in 1929, when the Lockport dam was only ten years old. Classic diner décor – shiny metal jukeboxes, booths, '50s and early Red Wings and NHL paraphernalia. Skinner's son, also named Jimmy, as well as players such as Terry Sawchuk were said to have worked shifts in this diner before their hockey careers took them away.

Skinner's will always remind me of photographs my husband took of Mom over the years. Lockport, a hot dog and a walk. A man and his mother-in-law.

Catherine Kennedy would have known the force of the Red River, but she died before the dam was completed in 1910. She wouldn't have known about the Red River floodway or watched as the St. Andrews rapids – the "Grand Rapids" in Reverend Cowley's map – disappeared under the teeth of heavy equipment.

Nor would our Everygirl, Annie, who follows travellers along River Road.

If Annie were here, we'd join the crowds now walking the riverbank – families with strollers, bikers, young lovers and Sunday gadabouts. The day feels celebratory, as though it's hosting a party to welcome summer.

We'd have ice cream, Annie and I. We'd sit and watch the dozens of Canada geese on the flats by the water.

We'd tell stories.

School

There was a time when all the people and all the animals understood each other and spoke the same language.
— Elder Betsy Anderson, Tadoule Lake, Manitoba

Every single one of us, Indigenous and non-Indigenous alike, has been fed a series of lies, half-truths and fantasies intended to create a cohesive national identity.
— Chelsea Vowel (âpihtawikosisân), *Indigenous Writes*

When I was twelve, I begged for a pair of mukluks, likely a gambit to fit in at the new school. When they weren't on my feet, they were by my bed, where I could sink my fingers into the fur and breathe in the smoky tang of the hide. In The Pas, Manitoba, snow came in high drifts and stayed for the winter. The leather soles of the mukluks were as flexible as socks, and I could hop from snowbank to snowbank to get to school, to meet my friend at the Cambrian Hotel on Third for a root beer and to join crowds at the Trappers' Festival, all with feather-light agility.

Fur-and-hide-wrapped feet were tucked under most desks, as I recall. My mukluks were pristine, so I scuffed them with gravel or dirt wherever I could find it. Miss Barbour was stern: in her British History class, I learned a whirl of names and dates that slipped my mind the moment I passed in a test. In English, Mr. Komenda gave us sheets of Latin and Greek roots; our task was to list all the English words deriving from them. Greek: *logos,* meaning *word, study.*

I sat at the side of the room, away from the teacher's gaze and in front of the quietest group, students who walked across the railway bridge every morning and passed my house along the banks of the Saskatchewan River. I was curious about their stories, not Cromwell's or Queen Elizabeth's. The teacher rarely asked them a question; it was as though they were invisible. They rarely spoke.

In town, they were called half-breeds, Indians. Later I would know them as Métis or Cree. They might have been members of the Opaskwayak or Norway House Nations. They might have travelled to The Pas, where they, too, would learn names of the kings of England, Latin derivations of *frangere,* meaning *to break, to vanquish.*

After I'd moved away, Helen Betty Osborne moved down from Norway House to live at the Guy Hill Residential School outside of

Helen Betty Osborne plaque at the site of the former Guy Hill Residential School outside The Pas, MB. Photo by author.

Following the River

The Pas, then to attend Margaret Barbour Collegiate Institute, now named after my former history teacher. I wonder if Helen Betty wrote an essay about the British North America Act, or filled in a sheet with language other than Cree. I wonder if she sat at the back.

Years later, I was in Winnipeg, the mukluks stuffed in a closet, my blithe and carefree youth behind me, my "Canadian" education in place. Helen Betty was abducted walking at night along Third Street near the Cambrian Hotel, stripped and beaten, driven to a spot near Clearwater Lake, beaten again, stabbed over fifty times with a screwdriver and left dead in the bush, her face smashed beyond recognition. When her body was found, she was wearing only her winter boots.

To identify her, they lifted fingerprints from her school books.

Latin *videre*, Latin *frangere*, Latin *mort*, Latin *cide*.

∾

The Great White way could silence us all
if we let it
it's had its hand over my mouth since my first day of school.
– Marilyn Dumont, "The Devil's Language"

∾

I can't seem to find it.

After a couple of weeks in The Pas, I'm still relearning the landscape I knew as a child. Renee, who works with Opaskwayak Cree women at The Pas Family Resource Centre, has given me directions to find the site of the residential school Helen Betty Osborne attended. Her death has haunted me, along with countless people in Northern Manitoba and beyond. Twice I've driven down the gravel road into the bush with no luck.

I turn back and drive to the convenience store near the airport. A woman emerges with a bag of groceries.

She greets me with a smile.

"I'm looking for the old Guy Hill property."

"It's no longer marked," she says. "Follow me."

About a kilometre away, she flashes her lights and gestures out the window to the road – the same road I'd driven down. Not far enough apparently.

The bush here tugs at my memory. When my family lived in The Pas, I learned to love northern skies, the forests, the rocky shores of lakes.

Now, decades later, as writer-in-residence in The Pas, I learn I will be staying at Clearwater Lake, about twenty minutes outside of town. I recall splashing in that cold water, remember horseflies as large as your thumb, egg sandwiches wrapped in waxed paper, ants, ice-blue skies. A day trip out of town to a sparkling lake surrounded by bush.

As a family, though, we'd never driven past the lake and this far into the bush. A few kilometres later, I reach a large field of birch and poplar, spruce, caragana bushes and the overgrown remains of tracks. I follow them into the field, stop when the urgent spring growth scrapes the bottom.

Ahead, a tree is dressed in fabric pieces hanging like a rainbow-coloured flower.

Nearby, a chunk of cement and a collapsed tipi, tied with blue cord around the tops of the logs. Camping? A place for fasting? For a ceremony?

It's quiet except for busy birds, my rustling footsteps and the wind whiffling in the birches and the tall grass. A cool, sunny day, capped with clouds.

This is the boreal bush. This is far into the bush.

But I'm still not sure I am in the right spot – I was told there was a memorial for Helen Betty at the old school site. Guy Hill was one of at least nineteen Manitoba residential schools under Methodist, Catholic, Anglican and Presbyterian oversight. Any of them could have housed my distant relations.

I back out, take the gravel road farther, turn a wide corner and there it is: a huge expanse of haunting absence.

I'm unsettled as I park the car, a bit jittery.

A plaque: *Guy Hill Residential School: 1958–1979.*

Beside it, a larger monument with Helen Betty's name nearly obscured with dream catchers and other mementos. An old bible, soaked with yesterday's rain. A St. Christopher medal. And Helen Betty's face forged in bronze. She was here for two years before she moved in with a white family in The Pas.

I touch the plaque, set in a circle of concrete on an angle, like a round bookstand.

The seam between the metal and the concrete is filled with pennies, tiny necklaces with crosses, a few small feathers. Stuffies, coins, a dream catcher, even a plastic headband sit about three deep around the larger base. Like the spot near Clearwater Lake, there must have been hundreds of people that stopped here over the years. Beside the bible are a few half-crumpled pages of printer paper: the ink has bled and blurred, but I can make out a few phrases: *missing person…marginalized…women…without fear of arrest…increase awareness…coordinate responses.* A student? An activist? A grieving family member who has found information about Indigenous women and the justice system?

Beyond, the field is embraced by the fresh, bright green, gentling hush of trees, all the wanton growth spring offers. Budding caragana bushes and their tender yellow flowers, the shape of plump crosses. A sweet treat I once picked on the way to school as a child.

Except for the monuments and the impressions of tire tracks, the site is abandoned. No leftover wire or old containers, no wood, glass, concrete footing or rotting boards. Only voices that have been in the air all along, voices joining with others', waiting to be heard.

We had to hold our hands out with books in our hands for a long time, saying Hail Marys.

They hit me on the head with a dictionary until I saw stars. I spoke my own language and was strapped so many times my hands were purple.

When I went home for a visit, Mom pulled up my shirt to see the welts and the bruises. My dad went to the school and after that the nuns picked on me even more.

And then after church, there was a little canteen in the church, and the priest would sell us candies. Well, after they got to know us, they started making us touch their penis for candy. They were there to discipline you, teach you, beat you, rape you, molest you, but I never got an education.

I close my eyes, hold space. Trees here were witness, this grass held small feet. This patch of earth has swallowed cries.
So beautiful a place.
So far from the main road.

∾

But She Cannot Learn the Meaning
— *A visit to a travelling exhibition in The Pas about Canadian residential schools*

Start with the positive, a curator must have said.
In the museum, the first display panel quotes
a woman from Cecilia Jeffrey School.

Following the River

She only speaks of learning valuable things, it reads –
cooking, cleaning, laundry, taking care of a home.
She cleans fastidiously, obsessively, her son says.
She has nothing out of place except

herself. What stain was she washing away? What
monster did she tame with hospital corners
and an immaculate kitchen sink?

Rub, scrape and shine.
Read the gospel. Scour
and polish. Scour and cleanse.

*And stood at his feet behind him weeping, and began to wash his feet
with tears, and did wipe them with the hairs of her head, and kissed
his feet, and anointed them with the ointment.*

Farther along the display corridor, Confederation
poet Duncan Campbell Scott, a man whose words
suggest an obsession with half-breed women, words
I would have consumed in school:

But she cannot learn the meaning
  Of the shadows in her soul,
The lights that break and gather,
  The clouds that part and roll.

Here, though, Scott's words fill an exhibition panel,
written not as a poet, but as the bureaucrat
who led Bill 14: *Our objective is to continue until there
is not a single Indian in Canada that has not
been absorbed into the body politic.* Much later,

I track down the son's fuller account. *Even my mother,*
he writes, *despite staunch declarations she had learned*
good things there, carried wounds she could not voice...
The school scraped *the Indian off their insides, and they*
came back to the bush and river raw, sore and aching.

Absorb. And be absorbed. Like red wine, grease,
rust, grass, ink, mud, smoke. And blood.

Just try to get those out.

Water: Stone: Woman

Forty-five years. Some here can go back to a Saturday
night with winter in its clutches. I come north
in the heat of May, buds opening on the alders, dust
clouding the road, four trucks with boat hitches parked

by the pumphouse at the lake where you were found.
New offerings since I last came – blue watch, red beaded
necklace, butterfly pin. Your name now barely visible
on the wood cross overlooking the water. Old ones in town

still remember; some kept silent for years while four men
hid in plain sight. One is the friend of a man I recently
met: I don't know what to make of that – too close.
Two, they say, moved to BC; one drank himself to death.

The one who went to jail was known for his loathing
of Indians, perhaps because his mother was one, and she
had left him. One family moved away, one mother – like
yours, Betty – outlived her child: both bearing misery

like stones against their hearts. And the father who
washed blood from his car afterwards, knowing all
the while what hands can do. I'd left town years before
they picked you up on Third, drove you here, pulverized

your young body: fists, a screwdriver, a boot, God knows
what. Your mother able to identify only your eyebrows.
A tiny piece of your bra strap found later in the car.
The fierce blue of this lake, hard water rushing against

the rocks, spring wind and dust, a riot of chickadees,
drumming of Northern flickers. I tuck a speck of earth's
memory, a stone from an Atlantic beach, into a fold of cloth
at the top of the cross, where it joins layers of offerings:

a stuffed bunny deflated from years of snows, rosaries,
silver coins, crumpled bills, whole unburned smokes, rings,
pins, lanyards, a hat, beaded necklaces, sunglasses, baby
shoes, gems, dream catchers, delicate gold crosses,

               a midden of woe
deepening like memories.
           Nipawin, iskwew.
              Spring wind in the vestiges
of spent love, the lake, alive, tumbling the sharp edges
of rocks and old grief.

The Road Back

When the women
spoke of their ancient grandmothers,
spoke of being outcasts.
– Louise Bernice Halfe (Sky Dancer), "oskwāpam – the pipe"

About an hour north and east of The Pas, static muffles the only radio station left, and then the sound cuts out. I may be driving in silence to Norway House.

Trees. Hundreds of kilometres of trees. Swampy patches. Gravel roads that lead to lakes. Pavement, then gravel, then pavement again, and a vehicle coming from the opposite direction about every ten minutes or so. I hadn't realized my longing to be in a remote landscape until I was inside it. Not trudging through bog carrying a child or hides or provisions, as so many have for likely thousands of years, nor struggling through snowstorms or clouds of mosquitoes or flies, nor on high alert for predators or food.

To know I have come from people who did remains a shock. I am sealed in a secure vehicle, my only frisson of worry the lack of a cellphone signal.

I approach Jenpeg and see a large creature in the middle of the road. I slow down, watching the bear lumber – they really do lumber – across and around a stopped transport truck. It's been years since I last saw a bear, and that was in the mountains. This one is large and lanky.

As I pull up across from the transport truck, I can make out the grey on the bear's face, its daggy fur, its rheumy eyes. I roll down my window.

"Food?"

The driver leans out. "Yeah, always a few of them around here. People keep feeding them."

The bear walks slowly between our vehicles and passes the front of my car.

"This guy here's well known," he continues. "I've seen him before, he's – ah!" He points past my shoulder.

I turn, and the bear and I lock eyes. His – or is it her? – dusty paws are resting high on the passenger door window, footpads cracked and encrusted. As we stare at each other for what feels like a full minute, I feel something shift. I grope for my phone to capture a photo but I am too late: the bear drops down, ambles around the back of my car into the ditch and heads toward the forest.

Êkosi, it might have been thinking. Or, dumbass môniyaw. Wêmistikôsowak, perhaps.

It has been a bright day. I set out early from The Pas, planning for a five-hour trip. Norway House has lived in my imagination for so long. I'm thrumming with the possibility I may be able to travel to Warren's Landing, walk along the water's edge where the SS *Premier* docked for the last time.

Manitoba poet David Williamson lives and works in Norway House. When we began to correspond about my visiting for a reading and a workshop, I knew only that Norway House was at the north end of Lake Winnipeg, and that Warren's Landing was where ships docked. Internet searches didn't help. Was there a winter road to Norway House? A summer road? Do people travel by float plane? Was anyone still living at Warren's Landing? I was full of the naive questions of a southerner.

Following the River

I have visited most of the other homelands of my past – Ireland, Scotland, France, Quebec, England, along with Ontario and the Western provinces – but Norway House and Warren's Landing seem more pressing, urgent. They are the missing pieces. Something, somebody is there – and it's not a belief; it's a kind of yearning.

Mortality is part of the pull, as cliché as that is. The post–World War II generation, wearing their fanny packs and sensible shoes, is now poking around in archives and museums, travelling to homelands, overrunning libraries and genealogical organizations, hoping to learn where they came from before their lives are over. The Internet has multiplied our interest in our ancestors – no one needs to travel to a church or a municipal office to pore through files and ask for a photocopy of the birth certificate.

At the time my grandmother Eleanore died, I was a novice teacher, incurious about the past and focused only on the future. When my maternal grandmother died, I was so caught up in child-raising and work that I'd lost the chance to hear her stories. And so, in my mother's later years, I sat with her and a tape recorder to hear her stories and try to preserve her voice.

No recorded voice of Catherine, though. And the only story of her I can find is the final one.

My feet will touch the land of her ancestors, though, and my hands the water.

The farther north I drive, the more alive I feel.

Crooked Tongue

When I cross over water at the Jenpeg Generating Station, I am crossing the Nelson River. This is the territory of the Pimicikamak Cree Nation.

The Manitoba government flooded sixty-five square kilometres of their land in 1977 to build a hydro station and agreed to compensate the Pimicikamak people, an agreement that – no surprise – wasn't honoured.

During a protest in 2014 that forced the closure of the station, Chief Cathy Merrick said the project "has turned a once bountiful and intimately known homeland into a dangerous and despoiled power corridor." Later that year, Premier Greg Selinger promised to travel to Cross Lake to offer an apology and a revenue-sharing agreement.

In 2016, the people of Standing Rock would begin to protest plans for the Dakota Access Pipeline to cross underneath the Missouri and Mississippi Rivers. I don't know this yet, but the protests will grow and draw support from across the globe.

The push for "progress" never ends. No wonder there is resistance.

Pimicikamak, meaning *people of rivers and lakes.*

Water: *nipiy.*

I get out of the car to breathe the air by the river. A bit piney, fresh, but with a faint whiff of diesel. This is the last part of the Saskatchewan and the Red River systems. If I step into a boat now, I could make my way to Hudson Bay. Or my body could – I'm sure I wouldn't arrive breathing. It's a complex route, the river system, and it's a brutal journey.

Following the River

I find a spot away from the bridge to watch the water.

Erasmus. Kennedy. They would have made this trip. And Henry Budd, several times.

During my time in The Pas, I've visited the Sam Waller Museum twice, first to learn about the area's history and again to reread the material about Henry Budd. A Henry Budd College for Ministry is in The Pas, where Budd spent much of his life. When I stood with my family at my youngest brother's baptism in Christ Church in the early 1960s, I had no idea the original church on the site was founded by him.

And no idea he was a great-uncle a few generations back.

The week before I set out for Norway House, I decide to visit the church building. It's a warm evening; the door between the church and its addition is open, and I hear voices. A man appears from a room down the hall and when I ask if I can enter the church, he seems delighted. He returns to what looks to be an AA meeting, and I walk into the dimly lit nave. It is smaller than I remember, filled with historical plaques and images, heavy with quiet and an air of gravitas that slows my steps.

I take in the homey atmosphere, the shock of colour from the stained glass windows, thinking again how drawn I am to old churches and graveyards. At the back of the building is a photograph of Budd, which surely must have been there when we attended church decades ago. At that age, I wouldn't have noticed or cared. Would my father have known his connection to Budd? I'll never know.

Frail threads – lately I'm struck by how easy it is to loop through time, see the past in new ways.

Christ Church overlooks the Saskatchewan River, and I realize now it's only a few hundred metres away from where we lived below the railway tracks those many decades ago.

Henry Budd was Kitty Budd's brother. He was born in Norway House to Wash-e-soo-E'Squew and Muskego Budd and named Saka-chuweskam, a name meaning *going up the hill.*

The author and family at Christ Church in The Pas, circa 1960.

Sakachuweskam.

The flies are getting to me, and so I return to the car and dig out my notebook. Yes, Sakachuweskam. I try to say it.

Original names, before Christianity and a foreign language took over. Peter Erasmus Jr. (my two times great-uncle) reportedly was fluent in six Indigenous languages, along with a smattering of Greek and Latin. He studied with his uncle Henry Budd in The Pas for a time, but was self-taught, too – he was young to be so accomplished. In any case, if any nano-speck of language-learning DNA from the Budd and Erasmus families managed to survive into the twentieth century, it swam past me.

For reasons of trade and survival, most people in nineteenth-century Red River would have spoken two or three languages or more. It might have been Michif, Bungi, Cree, Oji-Cree, French, Irish and Scottish Gaelic, Swedish, Indigenous languages from farther east or south, or an interesting blend of several. Unilingual British newcomers, who believed in the English language as a civilizing tool, must have been perplexed and likely fearful hearing such multinational conversations in their midst. With the power of the British Empire and the printed word behind them, however, they managed to stifle or bury many Indigenous tongues.

Today, an estimated sixty Indigenous languages are all that remain in this country.

Which did my grandmothers and their mothers speak?

Grandmothers. I check my notes. The word for *great-grandmother* is *Nitâniskotâpani-nohkom*. I think that's right.

I try to break it down phonetically: Catherine Kennedy is my "nee-danis-go-dapee-noow-gum." A *great-grandfather* is *Nitâniskotâpi-nimosôm*, or "nee-danis-go-dapee-nee-mo-soom." I'm not good at this. And the word for two-times or three-times great? *Nitâniskotâpani-nimôsôm*.

Cree women? That's easier. *Nêhiyaw iskwew*. No, *ininiwiskwêw* in this area.

The nation, however, is more difficult: *Nêhiyawak*. Or *maskêkowi-niniwak? Cree, Swampy Cree, Muskego, Muskegon*, I've learned, are all English words for the nation of peoples living around Hudson Bay and further south along waterways that connect to the Red River.

And in the museum in The Pas, I'd also come across a word I'd not seen before: *Ininiwak*. Cree scholar Neal McLeod reminds me this is a more accurate name for Cree in Northern Manitoba.

As I travel the last few kilometres into Norway House, I mutter the few words I know. Norway House – *river with a lot of fish*:

Kinosao Sipi. Kinosêwisîpiy.

Practise that.

Archway at the historic site of former Norway House Fort (built in 1826).
Photo by author.

Restless

I am surprised at how much green there is. What had I expected?

When I first arrive in what I think is Norway House, most of the deciduous trees and bushes are a soft early-spring green. Perhaps I'd expected a rockier landscape, like those of Northern Alberta, Nova Scotia or Newfoundland.

Houses dot the road, many with plain board exteriors, some with plywood. Dogs weave back and forth along the street. As I drive, I am not sure if I am in Norway House Cree Nation or the official town of Norway House.

Ha – what is "official" anyway?

Besides, Norway House didn't start out here. Not exactly. Failed settlements by the Jack River, then at Mossy Point and possibly Warren's Landing, then fires, disasters and out-migration to Red River and north to York Factory – all made settlement in the area, well, unsettled until the twentieth century.

But now, this settlement is no longer in my imagination. I am here.

First, I'll orient myself and then find the Lighthouse Cottages, where I'll be staying.

I pass a major intersection with a Salisbury House and what looks like an arena. I turn and follow a road – modest houses, more dogs – to what looks like the main wharf area. A meeting area is set up with chairs, and I see a long open boathouse – this must be where yearly York boat races are held. A large white church on the hill overlooks the water.

Is there more than one waterfront? I am aware of my southern expectations – a single waterfront, a main dock, a central spot for boats to tie up.

Across yards and driveways I see what I rarely see down south – children playing outdoors.

I can't shake the untethered feeling I have in this landscape. People I descended from lived and breathed here. Laboured here.

Peter Erasmus Sr., for one. Kitty Budd's husband. Catherine's grandfather.

In 1814, the post at Jack River was the main point for goods coming down from York Factory on the way to Red River. But traders were looking for more and better routes for shipping goods and for migration. Lord Selkirk thought a depot at nearby Mossy Point, at the west side of the outflow and near the opening to Lake Winnipeg, would be the way to connect routes.

And so, that fall, a Swedish man named Holte brought to the area a group of Norwegian labourers – some say they were convicts; others say they were freed prisoners of war – to clear the site and build the depot for £20 a year. They were a difficult bunch – rowdy, insubordinate and fond of rum.

One of them, known variously as Johan Frederick Swedson, Frederick Svendsen and, finally, Peter Erasmus, led a revolt over their working conditions. As a result of their bad behaviour, the group spent a long, hungry winter. The following year they marshalled enough energy to construct a building or two, and the Jack River post was moved to the new site.

Not long after, some of the men headed south to Fort Douglas and to the Red River Settlement. One of them was Peter Erasmus, along with his wife, Catherine (Kitty) Budd, daughter of Wash-e-soo-E'Squew (Mary Budd).

I like to think an ancestor of mine was a rabble-rouser – or perhaps simply a pain in the ass. Swedson/Svendsen/Erasmus and his wife,

Kitty, settled along the Red at St. Andrews, where they raised a family. It's still unclear whether Erasmus was Norwegian, Danish or Swedish – the HBC files, while helpful, don't always match up with information from other sources. More mystery.

But before Peter and Kitty Erasmus, many-times-great-grandmother Ke-Che-Cho-Wick and her daughter, Wash-e-soo-E'Squew, travelled these parts. I wish I could conjure up an image of their faces, their bodies, their dwellings.

After half an hour of driving along the river and following what I hope are promising roads, I find myself again at the familiar intersection with the multiplex and several stores. And the Salisbury House.

Chief Factor Bélanger on the wharf (circa 1890) HBC Archives 1987/363-N-46/1-25 Norway House-Transportation HB-14-00-2257.jpg H4-191-3-5.

No map, no cell service and no way to connect with anyone I know. And I still don't know where the Lighthouse Cottages are.

I park the car behind a group of houses by the river, next to two historic whitewashed buildings. One building is the old warehouse from the HBC settlement and one, I learn later, is the oldest wooden jail extant. I walk up the small hill above the riverbank and look down from the rocks to the Nelson River. Above and behind me is the single-lane bridge across to West Island. Below and to the left, a wharf and the Nelson River, the waterway that leads to Warren's Landing. Or, in Cree, to nêyawahahk.

This spot must be where the last and final post was built. It's a perfect vantage point to see incoming boats, and high enough to be safe. A cairn on the site identifies Norway House as the crossroads of the northern transport network of the Hudson's Bay Company. "Three structures – the Archway, jail and powder magazine – survive as tangible reminders of the importance of this place in western British North America." British – right. It's printed in both English and Cree syllabics.

Sophia Mason worked here as a missionary. Sarah Ballenden visited her friend Ellen Barnston, another "half-breed" wife of a chief factor. Harriet Cowan wintered in this town. People with means and, like my great-grandmothers, without. All have passed through here.

If there were a way for the scrim of time to rip away, for us to catch a glimpse of who and what has gone before. If I could walk to the end of the wharf below me now and greet passengers a century away.

I look up at the bridge to my right, decide to return to the car and cross over to the west side of the river.

I'm in luck: at the T-intersection, I see a sign for Lighthouse Cottages. Several kilometres later along a beautifully treed road, I turn into a driveway with a replica of a small lighthouse. A bumpy uphill climb to the entrance and I'm where I need to be.

After a chat with the owner, Lynne Mowatt, I drop my belongings inside the cabin and stand on the small deck overlooking the Nelson. A large king-cab truck is parked at the cabin next to mine. Below are a dock, a few water toys and a boat.

I watch the birds diving, notice the bullet blue of the water. The Red. The Hayes. The Nelson. Legendary bodies of water, passages for generations. No word I know expresses the feeling of being on land legendary for its stories, its significance. It's akin to looking up at the stars – a reminder of our ephemerality and the good fortune to realize it. It's a moment when time seems fluid, as though I could reach out and touch, see or hear an ancestor.

All I know now is that I am nearer, finally, to where Catherine died.

Before nightfall, I notice the setting sun catches the dirty paw prints of the Jenpeg bear on the window. I snap a photo as proof that a bear will rise on its hind legs to peer in a car window. I text my son the photo, tell him that today I've seen at least a half-dozen bears, including two cubs in the ditch.

That night, my sleep is fitful. I watch flickering green lights crawl along the ceiling around the smoke detector. Is it a light from another cabin, from across the water? Is it the wiring in this room? Is it my imagination? I recall newspaper accounts of the inquiry after the SS *Premier* disaster, the questions about its electrical wiring.

I am wired myself – overtired, anxious, my belly a cauldron of anticipation.

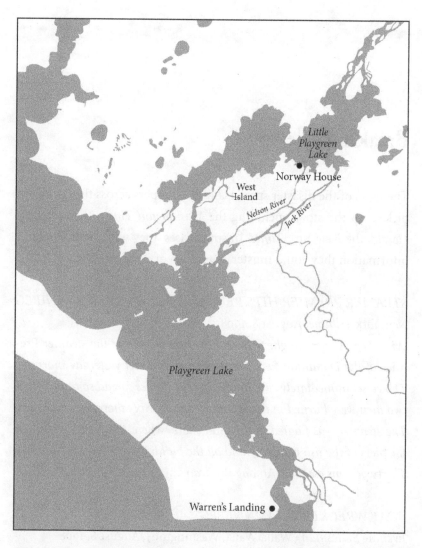

Norway House, Playgreen Lake and Warren's Landing map courtesy of
Kathy Kaulbach, Touchstone Design House.

Breaking News

The news of the disaster spread, and newspapers across the continent picked up the story, including the *Washington Times*, the *Salt Lake Herald*, the *New York Times*. In some cases, they went with whatever information they could muster, regardless of its accuracy.

STEAMER PREMIER HITS REEF AND BURNS NEAR WINNIPEG
New York Tribune, August 8, 1908
Winnipeg, Aug 7 – Eight persons lost their lives after the steamer Pre-mier of the Dominion Fish Company struck a reef yesterday morning. The vessel immediately caught fire and the flames spread so rapidly that two men were burned to death in their bunks. Six others were drowned. The steamer was floated and run to shore, where the flames destroyed the piers of the fish company and all the buildings at Warren's Landing. Thirty persons escaped. Among the dead....

BOAT WRECKER ON WINNEPEG
Evening Statesman (Walla Walla, Washington), August 8, 1908
Winnipeg, Aug 8 – Dispatches today confirm the report that the steamer Premier, one of the largest boats on Lake Winnipeg, was wrecked on a reef near Warren's Landing, resulting in the death of six passengers, and members of the crew. Fire broke out in the engine room [and] spread so rapidly that the people could not man the life boats....

EIGHT DIE IN BURNING BOAT
Coloma Courier (Coloma, Barrien County, Michigan), Friday, August
14, 1908 (back pages)
Winnipeg, Man. – the steamer Premier, *Capt. Stevens, was burned to the
water's edge at Warren's Landing, the northern terminus of Lake Winnipeg, Thursday. Six passengers and two of the crew lost their lives....*

The *Evening Times* in Grand Forks, ND, ran a story with more detail
and more accuracy on August 10, 1908.
EIGHT PERISH IN FLAMES IN BURNING BOAT
Steamer Premier *Burned to Water's Edge at Warren's Landing, Man.*
Cut Off By Flames in the Gangway and were Smothered
Selkirk, Man, August 10 –
*...the fire started in the hold of the boat near the engine room, and gained
such rapid headway that escape was cut off for many of those aboard.
The loss is roughly estimated at $54,000, only partially insured...Jones,
Overton and Fryer were three boys, who were on a holiday trip, as was
also Miss Povah of Winnipeg.... The dead are: Mrs. Antoine Couture of
Selkirk, passenger; Walter Olson of Gimli, Man., passenger; Miss Mary
Elizabeth Povah of Winnipeg, passenger; Elmer Jones, son of T. J. Jones,
manager of the Dominion Fish Company, Selkirk, Man.; Osler Overton,
son of William Overton, Selkirk, Man.; Leonard Fryer, son of W. T. Fryer
of Selkirk, Man.; Gus Weil of St. Boniface, Man., assistant cook....*

Inquiry, 1908: Safety

Commander Spain, Head
September 1908
Location: Assize Court, Manitoba

Witness: Phillips, Inspector of Steamboats:

"Did the Premier *not have a certificate covering electrical lighting equipment?*"

"No."

"Why did she not?"

"Well, she was fitted up before the act came into force."

"But the act was in force when you made your last inspection."

"Yes."

"Supposing the disaster was caused by the electric light?"

"I do not think it could have been. The wires were well insulated."

"Was Captain Stevens qualified?"

"He had an inland waters master's certificate. The mate had a mate's certificate for inland waters.

"The engineer and the second engineer both held a third-class certificate."

"How many passengers could the Premier *carry?*"

"Legally, seventy-five passengers. There is no limit by law, however, to the amount of freight the Premier *might carry.*"

"What about proximity of flammable material to heated surfaces?"

"*All such material was farther from heated surfaces than the act called for.*"

"*And the watchman?*"

"*The law does not require there should be a watchman. On long runs, the* Premier *has – had – a double crew so someone is always on duty.*"

Cousins

I wake to the sound of truck doors closing and the *bing* of a message. I'd finally fallen into a sleep so deep it takes a second to recognize my surroundings. I'm in a cabin above the Nelson River.

Norway House.

I look at my phone. It's David, the poet and teacher whose efforts have made it possible for me to be here. I'm not one to believe the universe aligns with our deepest wishes, but I'm grateful when it does.

After coffee and a shower, I am driving back along the treed road and over the single-lane bridge, much surer of my bearings. I pick up David at the campus building and we head for lunch.

Norway House is stretched out over small settled pockets along two rivers and a lake.

"Which is the town and which is the reserve?"

David laughs. "The area is divided in such a way that when you're driving, you can be in the reserve, then out, then in again," he says. We park in front of the Salisbury House and I recognize the big truck out front. It's the four guys from the cabin next to me at the Lighthouse Cottages. For those who can afford to eat out, the Salisbury House is the only restaurant in town. These men likely work for the province or the highways. Not locals, in any case.

David chooses a table near several friends of his, including another teacher from the University College of the North, and a man named Steven and his wife, Glista.

"This is the person who wants to get out to Warren's Landing,"

David tells Steven. Word must have spread. Norway House is a small community, like so many of the small towns I grew up in, and I always find comfort in this.

After lunch, we plan to visit the Hudson's Bay Company graveyard across the river – I'm eager to see names on gravestones.

"I need to stop at the Frontier School Division office first, though," he says. "I have papers to sign."

As we drive up in front of the small building, two women are lifting packages from the bed of a truck.

"Aha!" says David.

He turns to me: "Remember my telling you I thought you had connections here? There she is. This is who I want you to meet."

"Margaret." He calls to one of the women. "You two need to talk."

Margaret puts down the package and turns to me. As we stand there in the spring sun, her quiet smile draws me in. She is tall, distinctive, her long greying hair pulled back.

"You have relatives with the names Budd and Erasmus, David tells me. So do I."

I am thunderstruck. And ecstatic.

But why should I be surprised? This *is* where some of my ancestors came from – logic has it there would be relatives. Perhaps I simply didn't allow myself the hope of meeting one.

Instantly, Margaret and I begin to sort it out, and in a few short minutes of naming names, my wild hand gestures illustrating lineage, we have found our root connection: she descends from one of Peter Erasmus and Kitty Budd's sons, William, and I descend from one of their daughters, Sally. This makes us, Margaret thinks, first cousins four times removed.

Cousins, at the very least.

We agree to meet later, and I climb back into the car, shaken, grinning. And opened.

~

We park in front of a property near the shore with several mowers and other equipment out back. David and I head toward the trees and step over a chicken wire fence.

"This fellow does repair work for the school division." David ducks under a branch. A few steps later, we are in a clearing.

Years ago, David and other members of the community began to clean up the area. The Hudson's Bay Company graveyard had been overrun with weeds, tombstones tipped over, names barely legible beneath the rust-coloured lichen often seen on old stone.

I'm listening even though I'm buzzing with excitement about today's big discovery: Margaret. Suddenly, things are real.

"I still can't believe it," I say to David.

"I told you," he says.

I walk around, head bent, looking for familiar names. Jessy, daughter of Donald Ross, Chief Factor, married to Robert Clouston, yes. History comes to this – all those stories I've read about Ross and Clouston, and what remains? Stones, hidden and overrun with weeds.

Then, a few Budd names: Margaret Jane, daughter of Alexander and Nancy Budd. And Iliea Budd, five years old, daughter of Nancy and Alexander, dead eight years after Margaret Jane Budd. These would be very distant relatives, although I'd be hard-pressed to determine who's who.

Now, at least, I may know whom to ask.

We walk to the end of the graveyard and stand on the flat rocks overlooking the Nelson. On our left is the opening to Little Playgreen Lake. David points out Bull Island, named for the bull who gored HBC clerk Thomas Isbister. The bull was shot, Donald Ross ordered it taken over to the island and burned, and the fire destroyed both the bull and most of the island.

This spot on the Nelson, perfect for mooring a boat, is across and downriver from the jail, the Archway warehouse and the old munitions site. I'd stood on that site above the river only the day before, lost, trying to take it all in.

All the while not knowing I'd parked my car only metres from Margaret's house.

Budd gravestone, Hudson's Bay cemetery, Norway House, MB. Photo by author.

Inquiry, 1908: Missus

September 1908
Location: Assize Court, Manitoba

Witness: Antoine Couture, husband of Catherine Couture

"What do you remember of the night of August 5?"

"After I left my wife, I went to my room and went to bed. I was wakened up at one o'clock by the stewardess of the boat, Gertie Hourie. She was in her nightdress."

[The Winnipeg Tribune reports that "his eyes grew dim," and he teared up.]

"I came to the boat and saw it all on fire. And the top was caving in right where my missus was lying.

"I heard no warning, no bell or call of any kind except from Gertie Hourie. By the time I got there, many people had got away from the boat. No one was making any effort to use the pumps or extinguish the fire. I didn't see any living person on the boat. I saw the tug, the Idyll, lying on the far side of the Premier. I saw Captain Stevens and the second engineer on the dock, both of them in nightclothes.

"The engineer's neck was burned. The captain was making no move to do anything – he stood like a man paralyzed. He seemed to have just landed. And by this time, the wharf and buildings on it were already catching fire."

"When you left the boat earlier in the evening, were the electric lights burning?"

"Yes, they were."

"Was there a watchman on land that night?"

"There should have been. An Indian named Hart. Hart sometimes used to sleep on watch. I caught him asleep in the summer but I didn't tell the manager. He had an alarm clock and a lantern at his head. But I didn't see Hart around at all the night of the fire.

"My wife could only move slowly, because of a recent illness. Other passengers were able to jump through windows or over the rails or were taken off by other craft such as the Idyll and the Frederick. The fire travelled faster toward the bow – the wind was astern and this gave passengers in the stern of the boat an advantage.

"My wife couldn't have jumped."

Warren's Landing

Liz and I both try to grasp our hoods and pull them over our fly-about hair, but it is futile. Margaret and her daughter, Dana, are sitting at the other end of the bench, their heads down. Several times one of us tries to grab the flapping blankets and sit on them or tuck them under our legs. It is hard chop, the water looks like steel, and the boat slams constantly, sometimes lifting our rear ends a foot off the bench. I've had plenty of rough rides on corduroy roads, but this is the first time in a fishing boat.

We pass West Island, leaving Norway House behind us, and enter Playgreen Lake.

"Watch for pelicans!" David's voice is snatched by the wind and the noise of the motor.

It's happening. We are on the way to Warren's Landing.

We'd all had a late night at David and Liz's house, a celebration for the end of the school year and a send-off for a local teacher. Someone was pouring shots, my wine glass was never empty, and after a few raucous card games, lots of laughter, food and the surprise gift of a hoodie, I made it back to my cabin well into the wee hours.

David messages me in the morning to say we'll leave for the boat at eleven. I am groggy but elated. I leave my car at the Williamsons' house and climb into his four-by-four with blankets and a box containing a thermos of coffee and snacks. Margaret's white truck meets us at an intersection – her daughter, Dana, in the passenger seat – and they follow us to Steven's place by the water. Steven – the man I met at

Boat ride from Norway House to Warren's Landing.
Photo by author.

the Salisbury House with David – is part of the Norway House Harbour Authority, I learn later. Glista waves from the porch as we carry
our belongings down to the dock.

Outside of the shed where Steven cleans fish is a wooden bench,
much like the one we keep by the barn back in Nova Scotia. Steven
removes tools and ropes from it, rearranges a few things in the boat
and tucks the bench up against the back of the cab. This is our passenger seat – perfect. He must have cleaned the boat, I think, because
I can't detect the odour of fish, so familiar to me at home in Nova
Scotia. David climbs in the cab along with Steven, the engine engages
and we leave the dock.

Birds! The area is filled with rocky shoals, small islands with beautiful pale grasses, iron oxide on the rocks and carpets of water birds

261

– gulls and pelicans among them. We stop at Steven's camp, one of the many wooden camps on these tiny islands, more like rocky shoals, where fishers take their haul and clean it before bringing it into Norway House. The commercial fishing season starts soon and Steven has to prepare for it, but he's generously agreed to spend a day on the water with us.

Sometime during the windy, wild ride, I lose my hand warmers and Liz's hat blows off – the four of us in the back spend much of the trip laughing at our failed attempts to stay on the bench with our blankets and clothing intact. We stop briefly at Kettle Island, where we walk on rocks shaped like empty pots. The rocky shoreline, even on the smallest of islands or shoals here, reminds me of the south shore of Nova Scotia. Liz's sharp eye spots a goose nest well back from the water.

The day is cool but the sun is bright. High clouds seem to increase the expanse of water, the sweep of this land's shared history and my sense of how diffuse, yet strong, these new connections to my past are, and how they stretch me. Language, as always, fails.

We climb into the boat again and about a half-hour later, Warren's Landing is in sight.

Steven's boat is a basic, strong vessel. A contemporary one, suited to its purpose. It's not a tugboat or a York boat or a fifty-foot steamer. The water is choppy and we are all wearing life jackets, but a sudden squall, an unexpected collision, a nasty surprise could pitch all six of us in the drink. I dwell on that possibility, not because I feel unsafe but because I am in awe of generations of people who have made their way out into northern lakes in rudimentary vessels and treacherous conditions to travel from one settlement to the next or to bring back enough fish to live on for the winter. As survivors, acknowledging that hard life may be the only gratitude we can offer.

I turn my head to see Liz is crying. She's placed her hand over her mouth and is pointing to the buildings nestled inland from the shore, some of them fallen over, covered in new growth.

David tells me later that Liz, who grew up in Warren's Landing, hasn't been back for five years. Her father, who eventually moved to Norway House from Warren's Landing, died only recently. Known as PeeWee, he used to pilot the steamers from the landing through the channel to Norway House.

Steven shuts down the motor, and we climb out at a spot where remnants of concrete and wood footings suggest its busy past. Although it's a point of land, Warren's Landing feels like an island. Steven points south to show me the clearing on the horizon where Lake Winnipeg begins.

Margaret and I laugh as we wobble like penguins, trying to find our footing on the shore. We follow Liz along the beach, and then inland to the house where she grew up. There are weeds and overgrowth that are unfamiliar to me. Again, the search for names.

Tree suckers are wrapped around the steps to Liz's old house. Weeds pop up through cracks in the wood. We take the stairs gingerly and can hear the rotting wood creak under our weight.

Inside, Liz looks around and up at the ceiling.

"We have to fix this," she says to David. "We have to find someone to fix this roof."

She turns around, points.

"Look, there have been people staying here," she says, and is quiet for a moment. I wonder what memories of her childhood are racing through her mind right now.

"I'm happy about that." She takes a deep breath.

Rumpled sleeping bags are on the beds in two of the bedrooms. An old wood stove at the back looks to have been used recently. An ashtray full of butts sits beside a crumpled chair next to the front window.

We leave the way we came in, but Liz's foot goes through one of the steps, and when I follow, the whole step collapses. Margaret and Dana have wisely decided to leave through the back door leading to what feels like the town centre. When I walk around to the back to meet them, I can see the bare bones of a hamlet, of lives lived together. Each building is within only metres of another.

A whole community was here. Not only during the heyday of shipping and steamer traffic, but within the last decade or two. I learn from a booklet of elders' recollections that in the twentieth century Warren's Landing was the place some Norway House residents spent summers sailing and fishing.

One house within a few metres of Liz's former home belonged to Granny (Yvonne) Mowatt, who started a school in her house. I learn that Granny Mowatt and Lynne, the owner of the Lighthouse Cabins, are related by marriage. Later, a larger school was built further inland behind the trees. Liz points it out, but the path to it is grown over.

A meeting hall. A store. There is a kind of enchantment to this tiny community, with all its services nearby. A compact village, a perfect nest for children, with buildings so close you could likely hear someone in the store sneeze. And saturated with memories for Liz. I wonder if some of my relatives may have known some of hers.

We follow the path created by a four-wheeler. There is likely only one remaining resident here, Liz says, and that person comes only seasonally.

On our way back to the beach, Liz points out the old kitchen building and the bunks where workers stayed. Would that cookhouse building, now half-collapsed, be the one where Antoine Couture worked? His daughters?

Collectively, we decide the area up from where Steven docked our boat must be the old wharf area. A cross on an old cement platform commemorates the death of a young man, a Mowatt, who loved fishing with his father and his uncles. The community's loss was great, Liz tells me. It would make sense that the young man's parents would place his memorial overlooking the waters he loved.

As others move on, I stay to look at the old wooden footings and pilings – so many are charred or scorched. A lot of ash-coloured pieces of water-worn wood are at the edge of the water and in the weeds and undergrowth at the tide line. I caution myself not to make assumptions. Fires were common in nineteenth- and early-twentieth-century northern communities, and in some cases, still are. A memory flashes: our neighbours' house in Northern Alberta, up in flames with two of my playmates inside. The town fire siren, every noon.

One thing I can be sure of: Catherine's ashes would be in these waters. And possibly bits of the boat and the remains of other passengers. Perhaps the debris washed over to the Purvis Island side or sank to the bottom somewhere and has washed out to Lake Winnipeg or up the Nelson, joining countless atoms of the creatures the world's waters have claimed.

Ashes, bone, bits.

> *Those on shore were forced to watch helplessly as the* Premier *went up in flames. So intense was the heat that the hull burned to below the water line and the three-inch fire lining was almost entirely consumed. The vessel got adrift and burned for hours.*

Forty hours, according to the newspaper. There was nothing of her to bury, my cousin Edgar said.

We return to the boat, and Steven pulls up farther south along the shore to the spot known as Booth, where the lighthouse is located. We open the bags of snacks and the coffee thermos, David and Liz walk up to see the beacon a few hundred metres away and Steven, Margaret, Dana and I stay behind to look for rocks and stones, each of us picking our way along the shoreline, lost in thought.

Steven and I look at the horizon to the opening of Lake Winnipeg.

"That lake can be dangerous," Steven says. "The winds are fierce."

Inquiry, 1908: Ashes, Flames

September 1908
Location: Assize Court, Winnipeg

> Questioner: Mr. Heap, representing the Dominion Fish Company
> Witness: Arthur Andersen, Fireman

"Your duties, Mr. Andersen?"

"To keep up steam, keep the engine clean and also the stoke hole."

"Describe your actions the night of August 5."

"On that night, I slept up to twelve-thirty a.m., as I had not gone to bed until ten-thirty p.m. Ben Henreikson went to the fire hole with me when I got up and put in a fire. It was not five minutes from the time I left the fire hole until we saw the fire. I ran from the cabin at Ben's cry of 'Fire!' and tried to go upstairs, but the fire met me and turned me back. I ran onto the dock through the wood port. I saw no flames from the stoke hole. The fire seemed to be burning on the top side of the stairs. After I got on the dock, I shouted 'Fire!' three or four times."

"And then?"

"Then I went on the Frederick, and I got a line and threw it to the second engineer, who shouted for one. By that time the boat was all on fire amidships. I didn't see people getting off the Premier as I was busy helping the second engineer."

"At the time of going on duty, were the stoke hole floors clean?"

"Yes, I could swear the stoke hole was clean of chips when I left it. There was a little cordwood along the boiler. I emptied the ashes the usual way, and threw water on the hot ashes before they were hoisted overboard. I don't know if I did right or not."

"You were heard saying, 'My God, it is all my fault.'"

"No, I did not say that. I am a fireman. I never stay in the stoke hole – it's too hot. But I've never been told I am a watchman over the whole deck."

The SS *Premier* returns to Selkirk. "Remains of the hull of *SS Premier*." Selkirk, MB, October, 1908. Source: *Winnipeg Tribune*, October 5, 1908, p. 1.

Ship's Cat

holds magic in its tail, can call up a storm, ward it off.
Wanders through a ship keeping rats from the ropes,
mice from the crates of food.

Reads weather:

If frisky, then wind.
Sneezing, then rain.
Licking fur against the grain, hail is coming.
Restless, beware.

Stealthy. Furtive, crafty, self-protective creatures.

In August of 1908, as the steamer SS *Premier* passes the Spider Islands
on its way north to Warren's Landing, a mother cat takes each kitten
by the neck, throws it overboard and then jumps.

That's what happened, insists the grandson of the captain years later.
A bad omen.

"My grandfather was a hero," he says.

Montreal Gazette, October 19, 1908:
From the moment he was first aroused, [the captain] did nothing whatever – he made no attempt to give any alarm or to communicate with the engine room, but simply went into the wheelhouse and remained there till he went down to the main deck and then proceeded to get over the bow onto the anchor chains, from which position he was rescued by a skiff.

The court frees Captain Stevens from any charge of cowardice, but considers that at the time he lost his head and was absolutely useless as master of the vessel, and, therefore, considers that for this reason he is not a fit person to be in charge of a passenger steamer.

The SS *Premier*, still carrying the lower-deck passengers, drifts away from the dock toward a reef a couple of hundred yards away.

It floats, in flames.

"Sometimes Mother Nature has a way of foreseeing," says the captain's grandson.

"She speaks to us," he says. "Through cats."

Inquiry, 1908: Remains

September 1908
Location: Selkirk, Manitoba

First Witness: James Tait, of Selkirk, Manager for Dominion Fish
Company at Warren's Landing

"Mr. Tait."

"I was in charge at Warren's Landing on August 5. It was the last night
of the fishing and we were late clearing up. I left a little after eleven
o'clock. I was awakened by the watchman on the deck. He saw the fire on
his way back from waking the cook.

"I ran around to the west of the shed. I had no idea that there were
any passengers on the Premier at the time. I don't remember giving any
instructions to the captain of the Frederick. The tug stayed at the stern
of the Premier, using her hose, for about fifteen minutes. Both the Frederick and the Idyll were allowed to leave before the fire had burned out. I
believe I did all I could."

"Mr. Tait, weren't you asked to do all you could to recover the remains?
Mr. Couture has said that on the night of the disaster, you did nothing."

"I did all I could. A party of us went and rowed around the ship and,
with young Couture, we tried first to find the remains of Mrs. Couture,
but we could do very little until Mr. Cornish arrived with a pump from
Selkirk."

270

∾

Next Witness: Antoine Couture, husband of the deceased

"Mr. Couture. You have never seen Mrs. Couture since?"

"No."

"What was the second engineer doing when you saw him?"

"He was calling out. He was afraid. He nearly scared my daughter into a fit."

"Have you seen any of the remains of Mrs. Couture?"

"I have seen what I think were her remains. I could not identify them, but they were found in a position which made them seem most probably her remains."

In the Year 1908

The first unofficial Mother's Day is observed in West Virginia. Ladies' hose sells for fifteen cents. The wholesale price of tea is eighteen cents a pound.

Schoenberg begins his *Book of the Hanging Gardens*, changing classical music forever with its atonality, enraging listeners with its "noise."

A few months after Catherine dies, the Messina earthquake and tsunami will shatter Italy, killing 100,000 people in Sicily and Calabria. The same week the SS *Premier* burns, Wilbur Wright makes his first public flight, eight kilometres south of Le Mans in France. Later, the Silver Dart lifts off from Baddeck, Nova Scotia. In Walkerville, Ontario, Ford Canada begins to produce Model Ts, and in Prince Edward Island, MLAs vote to ban all automobiles from the island.

In Warren's Landing, lower-range lights are built between Lake Winnipeg and the mouth of the Nelson, one of the most remote beacons in Canada. Ogilvie announces its western division will include Winnipeg Flour and Oatmeal. In Winnipeg, the Icelandic Women's Suffrage Society is founded.

Back home in Selkirk, councillors buy Constable Hodgins a one-wheeled, two-handled paddy wagon to scoop up drunks harassing women at night, and one corner of Pearson's Hall is fitted out to show moving pictures. Free rural mail delivery begins.

The three-storey Selkirk General Hospital is built on land overlooking the Red, donated by Captain Robinson, founder of the Dominion Fish Company, who asks the area be named Idell. Idell (*Idyll*): the tugboat that sat alongside the burning SS *Premier* in the early hours of August 8, serving as a platform for passengers jumping from the flames to their safety.

The Way a Landscape Writes Itself

Language is less a human possession than it is a property of the animate earth itself, an expressive, telluric power in which we, along with the coyotes and the crickets, all participate.
– David Abram, *Becoming Animal*

Fishing Station, "Warren" Landing. Library and Archives Canada MIKAN 3371318. Credit: Canada. Dept. of Interior/Library and Archives Canada / PA-044893.

We want more than the world can deliver – evidence, hope, an echo of home. Charcoaled pilings jut up from the water along the beach; old logs and scrap lumber are strewn along the sand. Abandoned remains: a robot-shaped gas pump, a large yellow snowcat nestled in fresh green spring growth, a barrel-bellied '40s-style washing machine still tucked under the collapsed boards of a shed.

Fish – we are walking where the largest fish station on the lake once stood, where Lake Winnipeg steamboats docked. Over one hundred years ago, Warren's Landing was the site of massive wooden store-houses for fish and cargo, bunkhouses to accommodate fishermen, entrepreneurs, carpetbaggers and itinerant workers. Travellers disembarked at the landing before taking another vessel into Norway House; others, like Catherine, stayed at the landing, where they visited for a short time before returning south. Local kinosêwisîpîwininiwak such as Liz's family would have made a living out of the mix of commerce, tourism, fishing and storage.

Antoine Couture, my Quebecois great-grandfather, whom my father claimed was the owner of a boarding house, was, in fact, a cook working for the Dominion Fish Company. Catherine and Antoine's grown children were with him at Warren's Landing – two daughters who may have been cooks, housekeepers or clerks; and a son, Theodore, a dock worker, or possibly a jack of all trades. It's unclear if the daughters were Eleanore, my grandmother, and Kitty, back from the Klondike after the death of her infant and her husband.

On this day in June, more than a century after the boom years of trade in fish and furs, I walk with my friends and new-found distant cousins along the shore. At the edge of what was once a wide beach, trees, shrubs and grasses have taken over, pulling old lumber back into the soil. The dominion of the past has claimed footfall and voices, the whiff of woodsmoke and diesel, the odour of fish and the squawks of seabirds. Hands pulling the washing through the wringer, engines starting up, a fisherman refuelling at the pump – all ghosts outside our reach.

There are more ash-coloured wood scraps on this shore than I've seen on any beach or working dock. The fire on the *Premier* in August 1908 was massive – not only destroying the steamer itself, but damaging docks and warehouses nearby. A quick-thinking constable suffered burns retrieving a barrel of gunpowder from storage that night, likely saving the lives of people on the wharf.

The wafer-shaped piece of wood in my palm has been worn smooth. I rub my thumb on its softness, imagine its years of winters and springs, turned by ice, sluiced by waves. It's grey to the core.

When we consider countless horrors in the world, innumerable disasters and catastrophes, a ship consumed by fire on a late summer night is but only one. Unremarkable, yet its dark stroke colours lives for generations.

I steal a few minutes alone on the shore, examining stones, marvelling again at the urgency of the vegetation, struck by the magnitude of our long rivers of connection. It's a long way from the turn of the last century, and yet it isn't.

One evening years ago, my husband brought our infant son downstairs; moments later, an electrical short ignited the top floor of the house. Had our baby been in his crib, he would not have survived. It all happened so fast.

You were trapped, Catherine. Would you have heard the others in the first-class cabins above you when they leapt to their safety? Could you hear your husband or your daughter call out? Your son? Did they hear you? What could they smell? A fire so fierce you could be identified only by guessing the location of your berth.

What do I carry in my bones? Did my grandmothers imagine the future as I have tried to imagine their past? Yet I'm here – a fleck of their dreaming walking in the ruins, alive.

Trees are budding here at the top of Lake Winnipeg. The wind is light, the sun strong. Remains of the past at Warren's Landing – collapsed buildings, charred remains of wharves – settle into the landscape like another story being written.

"A thicket of many-layered meanings," as David Abram says, "for those who listen carefully."

As we prepare to leave the landing, Margaret and I watch the water in silence. I look south to the opening of Lake Winnipeg. I picture a steamer on the horizon, headed for this island-shaped strip of land, imagine passengers on the deck looking northward to this shore, waving, anticipating terra firma. Sons, daughters, husbands, friends and excursion agents will soon greet them. Antoine, Eleanore, Theodore stopping work to meet their mother as she disembarks from the SS *Premier*.

Standing with a cousin I did not know I had, drawn into a profound silence, I offer a blessing and toss a stone from a far-off sea into the water.

Part Four: Night Fishing

Night Fishing

Carrying fire, the two are silent as they tuck the spear underneath
the yoke of the canoe, raise the rolled birchbark to be lit and paddle
from the shore toward a cataract downstream. These years of wealth.
The torch draws dark apparitions toward the light, a stealth of mighty
sturgeon, leviathans whose origin reaches back to the Triassic,
over 200 million years ago. One holds the blaze, the spearman watches
the trembling surface and ties a line of sinew to the spear, takes aim.
The line spools, jerks, but he is steady, pulls the thrashing creature,
human-sized, bony-plated, up and over the lip of the canoe.

"So he yanked it to get the snag loose," she told the RCMP
later that night. "I honestly thought he caught a fish." The murk
in the Red so thick he'd guessed seaweed, but when she grabbed
pliers to pull the clump off the hook and he shone a light,
they saw it was hair, a mass of it, about six inches long, the size
of a fish. She tossed it back into the dark water, then thought
twice, picked the remaining strands off the hook, placed them
in a bag and called the police. "It's the North End," she said.
"It's sad to say, but not really surprising."

Blanket Statements

Alexander Ross, redux:

The blanket is considered indispensable; it is used on all occasions, not only here, but throughout the continent, both at home and abroad; if a stick is wanted for the fire, or a pleasure party is to be joined away from home, the blanket is called for. This habit gives them a stooping gait, and the constant use of the same blanket, day and night, wet and dry, is supposed to give rise to consumptive complaints, which they are all subject to.

Cheechum's words (through her great-granddaughter, Maria Campbell):

When the government gives you something, they take all that you have in return – your pride, your dignity, all the things that make you a living soul. When they are sure they have everything, they give you a blanket to cover your shame…all our people wore blankets, each in his own way… the blanket only destroys, it doesn't give warmth…. People would throw them away and the whole world would change.

Emily Kematch (residential school survivor):

I'm good at making a bed. We were taught how to make a bed perfectly. How to fold it, like each corner had to be folded just right and tucked in under the mattress, like the bottom sheet and then we put another sheet on top and our blanket. They were called fire blankets back then and our pillow and they had to be just right, or we'd get punished.

Of Middens and Graves

There exists an allegiance between the dead and the unborn of which we the living are merely the ligature.
– Robert Pogue Harrison, *The Dominion of the Dead*

My grandmother liked to cook and it was always she who cooked for us.... One morning she had made lots of bannock, and it was then, after noon, that she fell ill; and it was that same night that she died! And so it was her own bannock that was eaten at her wake.
– Mary Wells, "Fun and Games," *Kôhkominawak Otâcimowiniwâwa: Our Grandmothers' Lives as Told in Their Own Words*

"People ask me what my secret is."

Kay stabs at her salad. Her mouth wears a line of ranch dressing.

"I tell them it's because I was always doing sports. I used to skate. Play hockey." She laughs.

"I just keep busy, that's all." By now the salad dressing has moved itself into a different shape around her mouth. I imagine reaching across the table to wipe it off, but I'm horrified at the idea – the elderly are infantilized enough, and I don't want to embarrass her.

"And your dad. I was closest to him, you know. Not to my sisters as much."

"I thought you were close to Iona." My aunt Iona, like Kay's other sister, Lillian, was a tough woman.

Late in Iona's life the child she'd given up for adoption forty years before found her. She died reassured and happy to have met her grandchildren. And my aunt Lillian was no-nonsense, grounded. After raising five children, burying a husband and living for years in a small apartment near Kay's, with a yellow bird that sat on her shoulder, Lil died as her only daughter, Claudette, sang "Pack Up Your Troubles" at her bedside.

"Lillian and Iona and I got along, but Elvin and I were closer."

Yet he wouldn't speak to you for a time, I think. My father was furious Kay ended up with some of Iona's belongings. Another in the annals of petty family feuds. My father was my grandmother Eleanore's only son, Catherine Kennedy's grandson, an enigma and a source of pain to me and my siblings.

Much later, Allison will send me photocopies of material Kay wanted us to have. One is a note from Kay's mother, Eleanore, who died in the 1970s. The note is dark at its folds, and its faint script blurred even more by the photocopier. I can make out only a few phrases in Eleanore's careful penmanship:

> *My jewellery…hard to divide, but I believe Kay should have the ring with two diamonds…as it's her Aunt Kay's engagement ring…. My wedding dress you can decide…provided you think they will want it or deserve it…please save the $4.00 bill. I have never asked for help in money – once, but did not get it, so I've saved…the family [not?] to be having to pay for…do the best you can…please come and see me, write Iona and Iona [Elaine?] whatever news if it's good or bad…say some prayers for me.*

More than sixty years earlier, Eleanore had watched from the wharf as her mother was consumed in flames. And now she was writing from a hospital bed, preparing for her own death. So much pain she must have kept to herself, and so many questions we could have asked, but didn't.

"We skated all the time. Hockey." I'm startled into the present. Kay touches her plate.

"Eleanore?" Kay's daughter turns to her. "Ask them to wrap this up. I can't finish it all."

I do the math. Seven years' difference in age. Kay must have spent a lot of time with my dad. At his funeral, Kay stood, unsteady, in the pew farthest away from the urn while my father's widow, along with my youngest brother and his wife, chatted with mourners. She looked lost. I was caught up with revulsion at being in the same room as the widow and hadn't realized until then what a blow my father's death was for Kay.

"Let's take you over to say goodbye," I'd said. My sister, Kay and I had sat as far away as possible from the grieving widow. Allison and I helped her reach the urn.

Now, sitting in the restaurant for Kay's 101st birthday, I worry again if this is the last time I'll see her. Death for her is imminent, an incontrovertible statistical fact. She's the last of Eleanore's children, among the last of Catherine's grandchildren. We're all on the way to dust, I'm still nursing my anger and hurt over my father's betrayal of my mother, yet Kay is thriving. Although she always claims sports as her secret to a long life, I think it's her ability to let things go.

If one of a family Dies their nearest freind or Ralations Burries them Very oft'n with most of their Effects when Done is they put a pile of wood Like unto a faggot, round the graves, then they make an offering, putting a painted Stick up, some with a cross hanging a hatchet, Bayonett, or Ice Chissel, or what Else they have on the top, with the sculp of their Enemies, when they go to warr, which no Indians whatsoever takes away.

– James Isham, York Factory fur trader, *Observations on Hudson's Bay, 1743*

"They had a party for me last week, you know. In the block. Lots of balloons. Eleanore? Remember –"

Eleanore turns to her.

"Make sure you give those pictures to Allison and Lorraine."

The church of St. Peter has attached to it a burying ground....
Within this enclosure the rudely carved wooden grave stones bear
inscribed on them the strangely sounding names of many savage
converts interred under the shadow of this outpost of the Anglican
Church.

– Joseph James Hargrave, *Red River*

"You've been celebrating then! Did they have cake?"

But Kay is in reverie. "Your father and I skated a lot. He was a great skater."

"I remember that." My sister joins the conversation. "He was."

The server takes what remains of Kay's salad. I notice her mouth is clean. Allison turns to me.

"I used to skate with dad too. Dancing. You know, arm in arm."

"You did? You mean ice dancing?"

"Yeah. In Thunder Bay. I loved it."

Something about this pleases me no end. My father, labelled the Silver Fox by his railway cronies – the man who, on the night of his youngest child's wedding, told my mother, "That's it. I'm done." – must have cared for his children at some point. The image of my sister and my father doing laps around a rink softens me. He was tall and lanky, like Kay, and, apparently, a good dancer.

Rough calculations by population scientists show that, although
the current world population exceeds 7 billion, the number of dead
since the birth of the human race is over 107 billion people.

– Population Reference Bureau

Following the River

"One hundred and one. I never thought I'd get to 101. And I eat right too. I cook for myself." She nudges her daughter again. "Elea-nore, make sure you give those pictures – I've got too much stuff. It'll all have to be thrown out."

"Yes, please save them." Even as I say that, I know a stack of albums and clippings without a narrator invites a sorrow of its own.

To Aboriginal peoples, burial grounds are not archaeological sites, and human bones are neither artifacts to be displayed in museums, nor scientific resources to be mined; the remains of ancient ancestors are to be accorded proper respect. For many Aboriginal cultures, the belief that a spiritual 'essence' remains bound to the body after death means that remains should never be disturbed.
– Dr. Peggy Blair, Scow Institute

"Carolyn took me out for lunch the other day."
"What?!" Allison and I perk up. My father's widow.
"She complained the whole time. All she did was complain."
"What about?"
"Everything. That's all she does!"
"Is she still living where she was?"
I notice Kay's shoulders jut out more than they once did. Her sweater has a few stains. But her white hair is smartly cut, and she sits as erectly as someone half her age. My father hid his girlfriend from my mother for many years. What assets he had he put in Carolyn's name. But money wasn't the sticking point. She kept all the family photos, treasures our mother would never see again before she died.

The archaeological dig that prefaced the building of the Canadian Museum for Human Rights unearthed important evidence about the role of The Forks in aboriginal lives over the last 900 years. More than 400,000 artifacts were found and identified in two stages of the digs between 2008 and 2012…. Local aboriginal elders were consulted about the oral history of the site and how to respect the land being excavated. On the advice of those elders, a medicine bag was buried with each of the 500 pilings constructed to support the structure.

– Jim Bender, "400,000 Artifacts Dug up from Human Rights Museum Site" *Winnipeg Sun*, August 28, 2013

We create middens in our own small worlds. Objects and pictures saturated with memories that languish in someone's basement or are tossed into the trash, orphaned from meaning. An airplane's black box comes to mind – after a certain amount of time, it stops sending a signal.

But I'm not so sure. The stories may not be lost, just impossible to retrieve.

"Does she have a boyfriend yet?" Why am I even asking?

Kay half-grins. I think this question makes her uncomfortable.

From behind us, two servers appear and set down a piece of cake with a lit candle.

Kay turns but doesn't look at all surprised. Perhaps at 101 there are no surprises. Before the server's hand has let go of the plate, Kay has blown out the candle.

Learning

Swallows and chickadees bounce along the mounds of snow by the barn, picking at seeds I'd thrown out before the storm. Nova Scotia winters seem to be more violent each year. I am reading the report of the Truth and Reconciliation Commission and stop at the Executive Summary on education:

We call on the federal government to draft new Aboriginal education legislation with the full participation and informed consent of Aboriginal peoples.

And she comes to mind. The young woman in the GED program in the North who described sitting on the stoop with her mother one summer's end, feeling the city's heat, hearing sirens, watching her mother's glazed eyes as she tossed another cigarette butt on the pile by the bottom step. "I'm going to write a book," she told me.

– Providing sufficient funding to close identified educational achievement gaps within one generation.

I sat at her elbow as she bent over the foolscap, her face and arms mottled from fists, a knife, a BIC lighter. Her fingers flicked at the scars absently as she carved words in large, round script – the shape of surprise. Her stories, her words. Her healing, she says.

– Improving education attainment levels and success rates. Developing culturally appropriate curricula. Protecting the right to Aboriginal languages, including the teaching of Aboriginal languages as credit courses. Enabling parental and community responsibility, control, and accountability, similar to what parents enjoy in public school systems.

Eighteen, belly thick, hair bright red and braided, black roots an inch long. One hand moved to the ragged ends of her braid, then to the wall of skin between her baby and the world. Across the parking lot, snow was gritty, the surface pocked with the remains of chip bags and bent Tim Hortons cups. Beyond, a metal slide and monkey bars on the playground, sky the colour of pack ice.

Snow on the East Coast seems never to end. I think about language as culture and culture as language. About môniyaw principles of education: competition, standardizing, hierarchy, individual achievement, mastery of someday-you-will-need-this factoids packaged and passed on in books, testing (testing, testing), inside walls and in the head, a devotion to technology, compliance, the status quo.

As the birds dart to and from the feeder, fewer of them now, their shapes become indistinct against the white. I don't recognize the species, cannot name them, but it doesn't mean they're not out there in hostile Atlantic weather, trying to survive.

Enabling parents to fully participate in the education of their children. Respecting and honouring Treaty relationships.

Each time I sit beside a woman learning to read or write, I remember I have excelled in a school system that has ripped the beating heart out of another culture.

The young woman worked hard on that piece of writing. She said she could feel her baby move as she leaned into her story, impressing the page until her knuckles were white, asking me to spell *Montreal*, *amphetamine*, smiling as her other hand cupped her belly.

...to close...gaps within one generation.

Home

The red man was pressed from this part of the West
He's likely no more to return,
To the banks of Red River where seldom if ever
Their flickering campfires burn.
– "Home on the Range" (1910 lyrics)

Wet grass on the courthouse lawn, Prince Albert, my aunt Kay and my mother, my first steps. Nearby, descendants of Kennedys. Mistawasis. Northern Alberta, a long, dusty main street, railcars, the territory Erasmus travelled. A wire basket of library books, Saskatchewan prairie city, a bicycle over the Twenty-fifth Street bridge. East of here and long ago, an Irish-American immigrant finds a homestead and his son, a Red River girl, and they settle in Keeseekoose and Cote territory. All Treaty 6.

New mukluks and Latin verbs (Treaty 5, Opaskwayak). First date, steaming car windows, talking (Treaty 2). A morning's drive away, a wheat field tilled by Carson Glenn, Scottish great-grandfather, and his son. The son's widow and daughter settle in Winnipeg. Later, the daughter's family moves to Robinson Treaty area, returns. Bush, clear lakes, holiday cabins.

Begat begat begat – all those I claim: travellers, farmers, carpenters, nurses, itinerant workers, settlers, Irish potato farmers, Quebecois roundabouts, Indian agents, half-breeds and "full." Home is a river where Peguis was betrayed, is my orphaned siblings, my heart's roots, cloud ships of my youth moving across open prairie, the salty taste of the Atlantic on my tongue. Kitchens filled with grandmothers whose invisible hands hold mine, their names a benediction. Home is an empty vessel, a grief spoken beneath the words, is a small step into the day, longing for a shore. Is a promise. A nest. Is the moon, dark memories of pain, loneliness, fear. Houses we leave behind, land no one can own. Covenants we break and make again. Home is repair. Is work. Begin.

All I Need

"One hundred one and four months," I say.

"I know. Even my doctor doesn't believe it."

Near the end of the summer, I call Aunt Kay from the Fort Garry Hotel to arrange to pick her up for dinner the next evening. Again, I've spent several hours in the Archives of Manitoba and, tired and hot, have retreated to the small air-conditioned hotel room to go through my notes, reread documents, try to get my bearings. Tomorrow morning, a meeting with a scholar from the Louis Riel Institute and a trip to the Diocese of Rupert's Land offices before I head back to Nova Scotia.

When I drive up to the drop-off spot in front of the apartments on Worthington Avenue, I turn on the flashers, open the front and back passenger doors and head for the entrance. Through the glass, I see Kay emerging from the elevator, her head down over her walker, moving at a good clip.

Her plaid shirt is new; it's bright and crisp, and gives her the air of a superannuated, if very thin, lumberjack. Or the weathered owner of a northern hunting lodge. She's still handsome – stark white hair, intense eyes, high cheekbones. I can't bear to think of a time when she won't be here.

When we finally arrive at the restaurant – it's not far away, but we both lose direction – Kay is out of the car and pulling the walker off the back seat before I can make my way around to help. A customer on his way out holds the door for her, and I scurry to catch up.

This is Kay's favourite restaurant. I think its only selling point is its service.

Again, Kay orders the garden salad. Again, the dressing rims her mouth, and the dinner special is on its way. This time it's chicken and vegetables, with ice cream and coffee to follow. I settle for the restaurant's version of a Caesar: a small plate of brown-edged iceberg tossed in bottled dressing with a few black olives and tomato chunks.

Check your privilege, I remind myself. *What a snob you are.*

Kay sits back. "I've had a good life. Ups and downs. Like everyone."

No small talk with Kay.

"Anything you regret?" Even as I ask Kay this, I realize it's a ridiculous question. I want to ask her if she believes in an afterlife, but I don't. Does she think of a gathering place beyond our ken? Like me, Kay doesn't go to church.

"No. What would be the point? I can't change anything."

"Where do you want to be buried?"

"In Prince Albert. With Frank."

Uncle Frank died when Kay was still raising my cousin Eleanore. Decades ago. A jovial man with dark hair and complexion – I saw him last when I was about ten or so.

"Everyone's all over the place now." Kay has pushed the salad aside, waiting to ask the server for a take-away container.

"Iona is buried in Richmond. Lil is in Sainte Rose, with Gene. Elaine is in Washington. Your dad's in Thunder Bay. And Mom and Dad are in Kamsack. We're everywhere!" She laughs.

We are that, I think.

I'm reminded again of Kay's mother's bedside note to her daughter, its mention of a ring from another Aunt Kay. My aunt Kay had an aunt Kay? Of course, Klondike Kitty – variously known as Cate, Catie, Katy, Kitty and, apparently, Kay.

"I don't remember Prince Albert very well," I say. "But I do remember the photo of Mom and me –"

"Outside the city hall. I remember. I was there. You were my first godchild. We were excited about you."

"We went to Edson right after."

"I always liked your mother, even though your parents never got along. Frank's family was Native, you know. I told Eleanore she gets it from both sides!" She laughs.

The chicken and vegetables have arrived. Kay tucks in.

"I found a lot of information today."

"Yeah?"

"Catherine's baptism record for one."

"You're kidding! Where?"

"At the Diocese of Rupert's Land offices. February 13, 1859. Born in December, though."

Kay is absorbed with eating, so I sketch out a quick genealogical outline in my notebook – all the grandmothers – and turn it around to show her.

"We began here," I say. And I try to explain it from Matthew Cocking and Ke-che-cho-wick on down. I repeat the names a few times. Kay's hearing isn't getting any better.

"Seven generations of us."

"What? You're kidding!"

"I went to Norway House this summer. To Warren's Landing, where the steamboat burned."

Kay looks at me, her eyebrows raised.

"Look." I pull up the images I loaded on the tablet and scroll through them.

"This is where Catherine died. Your grandmother." She knows this; why am I reminding her?

"You went there?"

"It's close to an hour by boat from Norway House. With stops."

Kay is now more than twice as old as Catherine was when she

perished. And I realize this is the first time in years I've had time alone with Kay.

"I never knew Grandma," she says. "I wasn't born yet. And Mother would never talk about her."

No wonder, I think.

"Did you see Antoine much – your grandfather? Couture?"

"Not really. When we'd go to Selkirk, I'd visit Joan or Edgar or my other cousins. Grandpa was a nice man, though."

And a rascal, too, I think.

"You have some too." Kay's ice cream has arrived and she hands me a spoon. As we dip into the bowl, I catch the server's eye.

I nod my head toward Kay. "Not bad for 101, right?"

"Are you serious?!" She shakes her head and mouths *wow*. Kay is focused on the ice cream and doesn't look up.

"I gave all my plants to Ray and Shirley, you know. For their cottage. I was tired of keeping them up."

"From your balcony? It used to be filled with plants."

"Say again?" She shakes her head. "My hearing aid broke and I can't be bothered getting a new one. And I'm not spending that kind of money."

"What are they now?"

"Over two thousand dollars. I can get by. I have all I need."

Two hours of conversation about my family – "When is David going to get married?" "Where is Jesse working?" – and her daughter, Eleanore, and her dogs; about Kay's former work at car dealerships in Alberta; reminiscences of her sisters, Lil and Iona – especially the joy of Iona's finding her "illegitimate" son and his family – a report from Kay's doctor – "he thinks I have a couple more years"– and I can see she is beginning to flag.

When I park the car in front of the block on Worthington, I pull the walker from the back seat and unfold it. Kay grabs the handles.

"Wait!" I reach in for my phone and tuck in beside her.

"I've never done this before, have you?" I tinker with the setting.

We both grin at the screen. "Ha! I'll send this to you."

"I'm proud of all this work you're doing." She reaches up to hug me. "Love you."

I stand in the cool air and watch through the glass until she's through the security doors, into the elevator, and the door has closed behind her.

By Water

I think sometimes about old painters – they get so simple in their means.
Just so plain and simple. Because they know they haven't got time.
– Ursula K. Le Guin

She watches how
river waves fold
into each other
like family.
– Katherena Vermette, "family," *North End Love Songs*

Before I leave Norway House, Margaret and I arrange to meet. Who knows when I'll be back? I sleep hard the night before but wake briefly – someone is pacing outside the door. I don't recall hearing the neighbours' truck. When I peek out the window, it is so dark I can't see a thing.

In the morning, I open the door to take my things to the car and see garbage all over the deck.

So, a bear.

It is a cool morning, and damp. The river looks colder today. I knock on Lynne's door to pay my bill, and we chat briefly about Warren's Landing. Her second-hand store is full of gems, and I can't help staying to look at old glass and local artifacts.

When I pick up Margaret at the store near her house, she directs me to a road that leads to the hospital. We park and walk into the bushes overlooking the river.

"It's behind here," she says, "but it's all grown over." As we pick our way through bush and rocks, I see the remnants of a stone wall.

"They kept the munitions far away from the warehouse and the jailhouse. This used to be a large square." Margaret gestures toward the jail, then behind us, then to the right. "Everything was in here, the chief factor's house, the warehouse, all of it."

Kitty Budd would have lived around here. Her mother, Mary, too. Mary's son, Henry Budd. And Margaret's ancestors, as well. So many others. I am looking at a stone wall they would have seen, standing by waters they travelled. From Hudson Bay to here, down through Lake Winnipeg, the Hayes River, then to the Red – an ancestral umbilical cord. The old ones. The ones whose spirits we carry.

Only silence seems adequate.

Margaret points toward the spot downriver where I'd stood the day I arrived. "The dock area is higher up and people could see boats coming. Someone would shoot off a gun or play bagpipes, and everyone gathered at the dock."

Docks. Water. Passages. Time. Stories.

～

Several months later, it's a hot windy day in Nova Scotia, and I watch two pigeons waddle down the steep slope of the barn. When they reach the edge, they jump, their wings opening, it seems, as an afterthought. As children in Northern Alberta, my friend and I leapt off roofs of any coal shed we could find, using our tender arms for balance. That's decades ago, but I still remember the feel of the drop, the jolt to my legs. I was new to the world and such experiences, like scratch marks on wet clay, can make lifelong impressions. Strange what stays in the body as memory. My parents never knew what Darlene Nadarak and I did when we disappeared down the town's alleys until sunset.

A small moment, watching birds by the ocean, and I've fallen again into a distant present. I'm beginning to understand that all time is now. Everything washes up, recedes, washes up again.

Later in the day when the air cools, the dog and I walk down to the shore where the vetch and mustard are thick and high. Twenty years ago, it was a different shore and a different companion, a beloved animal we buried by the garden at the old house. But finding a path through bushes to the water – that's the same pull, and always has been. The edge of water is a magnet.

Shores. Sand. One day the Atlantic leaves a piece of blue glass, the next day, after a storm, a large log by the path has disappeared, possibly to turn up on the beach kilometres away. Or sink to the bottom of the ocean.

Summer is leaving. Something leaps in my chest when I see these plants at their peak, blooms ready to go to seed. Each turn around the sun – fewer now for me – and their appearance is more poignant, regardless of how familiar they are. Sea violets, pea flowers, buttonbush – oceanside species thousands of years old.

It's low tide and the water is pulling back, aroused by the moon. The sun is setting. Tonight, I will imagine the sea, the ruche of waves as they turn inside out, endlessly, like memories, like the past. Keats was right: all our lives are "writ in water."

I think of Margaret and her daughter walking by the river in Norway House, of Catherine on the banks of the Red, of grandmothers and all the old ones, their strong hearts, and the past wraps the present into a dream, calling me in.

tha uisge na beatha
l'eau est la vie
nipiy ôma pimâtisiwin

CELEBRATIONS

PLEASE COME AND HELP
CELEBRATE THE 102
GLORIOUS YEARS
OF   KAY RENAUD
        REYNAUD

SUNDAY April 30
1:30 to 3:30 p.m.

COFFEE, TEA and
REFRESHMENTS
WILL BE SERVED

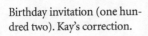

Birthday invitation (one hundred two). Kay's correction.

Aunt Kay (Kay Reynaud, Catherine's granddaughter). Photo by author.

Afterword

During the final months of completing this manuscript, the world of Canadian literature was rocked by several polarizing and divisive debates. What does and does not constitute appropriation is central to these debates, as is the related issue of who can tell whose stories.

Poet Gregory Scofield offers important insights:

...the idea of appropriation and the use of Indigenous knowledges, colonial trauma and violence, etc., has become neatly wrapped in a box called reconciliation, which if we are truthful is really about absolution and denial.... I deny no one their creative right to stories and to story-telling. I honour and respect those genuinely interested in Indigenous history and a commitment to moving forward, to collectively rewriting a history that has been inaccurately told and presented. But I also ask, with respect, that as Indigenous writers we are granted the right to challenge how our stories, our lands, our languages, our sacred stories, our healing stories, our teaching stories, our world views and spiritual/cultural practices are being 'mined' to further 'authenticate' a writer's work. Think in terms of the old-time anthropologists...[who] came with their shovels and notebooks.... They left holes in the earth where bones had been...

When I began this research on the death of my great-grandmother near Norway House, I quickly realized the depth of my responsibility. I have Indigenous roots, yet the stories of my six generations of grandmothers from Red River and north to Hudson Bay were never passed down to me. A colonial mindset held sway in my upbringing, permeating all I have come to know – it's the air I breathe.

Following the River

Although I began this research to learn the details of what seemed like an apocryphal family story about a fire, I was soon immersed in Red River history, hooked on finding more information about women whose lives have been ignored, disdained and dismissed in "Canadian" history. The more I learned about my "half-breed" grandmothers, the more I wanted to know about their contemporaries.

With no community to approach about my grandmothers' stories, I drew on as many resources as I could: books and newspaper articles from the last century and a half (largely written by white settlers), poetry and fiction by contemporary Indigenous writers, archival documents, community histories and discoveries I could make using my own two feet. I set off for the places my ancestors lived in – Red River (Winnipeg, St. Andrews and St. Peter's) and north to The Pas, Norway House and Warren's Landing – to experience for myself the landscape, burial grounds, flora and fauna, and places of worship, as well as the waters across which these women travelled.

Print material has rarely afforded Indigenous women the basic respect of a name, in whatever language. Generic names for women (the reader will recall names George Simpson was fond of using, such as "bits of brown" or "the commodity") were often derogatory. When I did find the rare historical anecdote about a nineteeth-century Red River woman, it was usually in relation to her husband's stature in the community. Racist, sexist and classist structures ensured that women of mixed descent became targets of Victorian faux probity and were thus considered notorious, morally depraved or uppity.

All the women in this book did have names, however, even though they may be unrecorded or beyond our reach. We are standing on their contributions.

All the while I searched for traces of my ancestors and their peers, I was using skills I gained over several years as an ethnographer in the areas of literacy and gender. Most useful to me were an ingrained understanding of context and a dogged persistence to find one more detail to help paint a picture. As readers will know, ethnography is the study of cultures – a branch of anthropology that has, as Gregory Scofield says, rightly earned a bad reputation in Indigenous cultures. I come from a generation of ethnographers averse to the belief in a "god's-eye view" of anything or anyone, who believe all research demands humility and openness. Over the years I've worked with women from a wide range of cultural backgrounds; overwhelmingly, their concerns are about voice and agency. My grandmothers and other nineteenth-century Red River women are no longer able to speak or act for themselves, but what few stories remain can, and do.

These Red River women reach from the past, put me to work and continue to show me the barriers and struggles they navigated. They marshalled resilience and courage to survive in a country invaded by ambitious and power-hungry Europeans with a lust for land, re-sources, riches, dominance and, yes, "dusky" women. All in the name of expansion or progress. Others' descriptions of these women expose both the women's palpable strength and the ugly roots of how they are treated. Forty-five years ago, Maria Campbell's groundbreaking memoir *Halfbreed* revealed hard truths. Today, I am in awe of the many ways Indigenous women continue to persist; resist; speak the truth; create life-changing art, literature and music; and lay claim to respect they've been long denied. To paraphrase Grace Paley, when you illuminate what's hidden, that's a political act.

At a time when awareness of Canada's destructive relationship with Indigenous peoples is growing, a time when resistance is forcing change, I welcome the grief and responsibility that come from diffi-cult knowledge. What comes with grief is a kind of solace, too, as we accept what we have silenced and resolve to address it. Tracey Lind-berg asks what might change if we were to engage with each other, to care for one another, as if we are all relatives.

Following the River

I am grateful beyond measure for having descended from remarkable women, to glimpse the world they inhabited, and as I continue to learn, I will walk with their voices inside me, listening for their wisdom.

Acknowledgements

My gratitude and respect go first to the Indigenous women whose stories are the centre of this work. Each of you is a light into the past and your lives continue to teach us all.

Thanks to members of my birth family, especially the intrepid (now 102-year-old) Katherine Couture Reynaud (Aunt Kay) and my sister, Allison Marion. To my brother Brian Boggs; cousins once removed Edgar Couture, Eleanore and Joan; first cousin Eleanore; and to Ray and Shirley. I'm grateful to new-found relations in Norway House, Margaret and her daughter, Dana, for their help and friendship.

Thank you to the staff at the Archives of Manitoba in Winnipeg, Manitoba, in particular, Monica Ball and Jason Woloski. Thanks to Nathan Kramer for his help navigating the archives, and to Maureen Hunter, Bruce Cherney, Ken Howard and Ruth Ann d'Entremont. The Pas Regional Library Board, Lauren Wadelius, Bev Bastien and Bonnie White were generous hosts during my time as writer-in-residence in The Pas and Northern Manitoba. Huge thanks to Lauren Carter for the vision, support and hard work that made the residency possible.

To Brenda Schmidt and the Ore Samples reading series, to University College of the North in The Pas, Dean David Williamson at UCN in Norway House and to The Pas Family Resource Centre and Renee Kastrukoff for opportunities to meet and work with writers.

Thanks to Wendy at St. Peter Dynevor Stone Church; her kindness has been a highlight. Ann-Margaret Day-Osborne and her family, along with Liz Williamson and Maria Sinclair provided essential help with Swampy Cree dialect. Miigwech, kinanâskomitin tâpwê. And without David and Liz Williamson's gracious help and hospitality, I would not have been able to visit Warren's Landing. Much gratitude to Steven Robertson for taking us.

I was fortunate to have perceptive readers as this book developed. These include Carol Bruneau, Julie Vandervoort, Binnie Brennan, Ramona Lumpkin, Norma Jean Hall, Kim Pittaway, Allison Marion, Sarah Scout, Jane Silcott, Cathy Ostlere and especially Don McKay and Fred Stenson. Norma Jean Hall's encyclopedic knowledge of Red River kept me on solid ground. I am grateful to Louise Bernice Halfe (Sky Dancer) for her wisdom, support and friendship. Gregory Scofield's open-hearted insights are a gift, as are conversations with Shelagh Rogers about kinship.

Chance conversations with Robin McLachlan (Australia), Kirk Couture (Canada) and third cousin Robert Couture (Washington State, US) filled in missing information. Thanks especially to Robert for his Couture files. Lawrence Barkwell at the Louis Riel Institute gave generously of his time and his writing on Indigenous women. Greg Younging shared his deep knowledge of Indigenous issues in publishing. I thank Marilyn Dumont for her kind support when I first began, years ago, to write about my ancestry.

The unflappable Noelle Allen has championed this book from the outset – endless thanks. The Wolsak and Wynn production team, as well as editor Emily Dockrill Jones and designer Marijke Friesen, are a force. Thank you to the peerless Kathy Kaulbach for maps.

This work has benefited from hundreds of conversations over several years with countless people and if I have failed to acknowledge anyone for their support, I apologize. All errors and omissions are mine alone.

My family has seen me through years of books and drafts and research trips and has taken it all in stride. To my husband, Allan, who means everything – thank you for being my rock.

Appendix

The Grandmothers: All My Relations

Ke-che-cho-wick (great-great-great-great-great-grandmother)
born circa 1758
most likely born in the Severn region near Hudson Bay
– country wife of Matthew Cocking

Wash-e-soo-E'Squew Cocking (great-great-great-great-grand-mother)
born in 1780, daughter of Matthew Cocking and Ke-che-cho-wick
likely born in the Severn region near Hudson Bay
– wife of Muskego Budd
– baptized in Red River as Mary Budd

Catherine (Kitty) Budd Erasmus (great-great-great-grandmother)
born in 1805, daughter of Wash-e-soo-E'Squew (Mary) and Muskego Budd
born in Norway House; migrated to St. Andrews; died in Prince Albert, Saskatchewan
– wife of Peter Erasmus Sr.
– sister of missionary Henry Budd
– mother of Peter Eramus Jr. (explorer and translator)

Following the River

Sally (Sarah) Erasmus Kennedy (great-great-grandmother)
born circa 1830, daughter of Kitty Budd Erasmus and Peter Erasmus Sr.
born in Red River (most likely St. Andrews)
– wife of Antoine Kennedy, member of Henry Prince band (Peguis)
– niece of Henry Budd
– sister of Peter Erasmus Jr.
– mother of Catherine, Ann, Jane, John and others

Catherine Kennedy Couture (great-grandmother)
born in 1858, daughter of Sally Erasmus and Antoine Kennedy
born in Red River; died at Warren's Landing, Manitoba, in 1908
– wife of Antoine Couture
– mother of eleven children, including Eleanore

Eleanore Couture Boggs (grandmother)
born in 1886, daughter of Catherine Kennedy and Antoine Couture
born in Selkirk, Manitoba; died in Winnipeg, Manitoba, in 1972
– mother of Katherine (Kay), Elvin, Lillian, Iona and Elaine
– wife of Charles Boggs
– aunt to current Selkirk residents Eleanore, Edgar and Joan

Other Relations
Katherine (Kay) Boggs Reynaud (aunt)
born in 1915, daughter of Eleanore Couture and Charles Boggs
born in Kamsack, Saskatchewan
– widow of Frank Reynaud
– mother of Eleanore (third of three Eleanores)
– cousin of Selkirk residents Eleanore, Edgar and Joan (also Catherine's grandchildren)
– aunt to Lorri, Allison, Brian and Ron, among others

Edgar Couture (first cousin once removed)
born in 1920
born in Selkirk, Manitoba
– grandson of Catherine Kennedy Couture
– cousin of Kay Boggs Reynaud

Margaret (fourth cousin)
– great-great-great-granddaughter of William Budd (brother of Kitty
Budd Erasmus)
– mother of Dana

Lorri, Allison, Brian, Ron (the author and her siblings)
– great-grandchildren of Catherine Kennedy Couture

*Note: Here I'm using "all my relations" in the limited sense of relatives,
of family connection, rather than the larger (more accurate) meaning of
connection among all plants, animals, rocks, water and natural forces.*

Notes

Some of these historical accounts have inconsistencies in spelling and usage, along with discrepancies in names, dates and perspectives; this is consistent with their eighteenth- and nineteenth-century sources. Passages are used verbatim without the use of *sic*; occasionally slight changes (punctuation, the addition of a single word) have been made to clarify meaning. I have used the word *testamentum* throughout the book to refer to statements and assessments written by (largely European) men on subjects affecting Indigenous people, primarily women.

Opening Epigraphs

Dumont, Marilyn. "the dimness of mothers and daughters." *Green Girl Dreams Mountains*. Lantzville, BC: Oolichan Books, 2001. p.23.

Solnit, Rebecca. *The Mother of All Questions*. Chicago: Haymarket Books, 2017.

Selkirk, Manitoba, August, 1908

Names such as Swampy Cree, Ojibwe and so on are names Europeans gave Indigenous nations, not names the nations ascribed to themselves. Names in Cree dialects included in this manuscript are in Roman orthography, not in Cree syllabics.

In many official records, the name is Warren Landing, but Warren's Landing, the locals' preferred name, will be used throughout.

Following the River

Introduction
Woman on the River

Description of the woman is excerpted from Keating, William H. *Narrative of an Expedition to the Source of the St. Peter's River, Lake Winnepeek, Lake of the Woods &c. &c.*, vol. 2. Philadelphia: H.C. Carey and I. Lea, 1824. pp. 69–70.

A Cord, However Slender

I am grateful for email conversations with poet Gregory Scofield, Red River historian Norma Hall and poet Louise Bernice Halfe (Sky Dancer). Their comments here are used with permission.

Passages Northwest

Epigraph from Hogan, Linda. *Dwellings: A Spiritual History of the Living World*. New York: Touchstone Books, 1995. p. 159.

Several lines in this poem were drawn from the author's earlier poem "Passage: Northwest" published in *Arc* 72, 2013.

In Between

Bev Sellars' comments about a homeland are from her book *They Called Me Number One*. Vancouver: Talonbooks, 2013. p. 190.

Christine Welsh's comments about a code of silence appear in her essay "Women in the Shadows: Reclaiming a Métis Heritage" in *New Contexts of Canadian Criticism*. Ajay Heble, Donna Palmateer Pennee and J.R. Struthers (eds.). Peterborough, ON: Broadview Press, 1997. p. 60.

The term *Métis* refers to a distinct group of Indigenous people whose identity has its roots in the Red River Settlement. A longer explanation can be found on Chelsea Vowel's (âpihtawikosisân's) site: http://apihtawikosisan.com/2011/12/youre-metis-so-which-of-your-parents-is-an-indian/.

Ta-Nehisi Coates's comments about race are from his book *Between the World and Me*. New York: Random House, 2015. p. 7.

Naming is a contentious issue. Despite extensive research, I may have misconstrued names and references for Indigenous communities (either historical or contemporary), and I accept full responsibility for any errors. I recommend Chelsea Vowel's book *Indigenous Writes* (Winnipeg: Portage and Main Press, 2016) for its thorough and clear explanations, not only about terminology and names, but also about current Indigenous issues and perspectives.

Hearing the Music
Of the many versions of the classic song "Irishman's Shanty," this is the one my father sang to us.

Part One: Setting Out
Driving North
Roderick MacBeth writes about Lord Selkirk in chapter 3 of *The Romance of Western Canada*. Toronto: William Briggs, 1918. pp. 26–27.

Crossing Waters: Notes and Recollections
The Hayes River system from York Factory was a key trade route for the Hudson's Bay Company in the late eighteenth and early nineteenth centuries.

Red River, 1860
News article from the *Nor'wester*, Thursday, June 14, 1860, p. 38.

Red River, 1862
Letter from the *Nor'wester*, September 11, 1862, pp. 38–39.

Following the River

Lake Winnipeg, August 1906
Material here is drawn from an article by Bruce Cherney, June 1, 2007, "Tragic Sinking of SS *Princess*," *Winnipeg Real Estate News, Selkirk's 75th Anniversary* (community publication), among other sources. Fireman George Freeman is quoted from the *Minnedosa Tribune*, September 6, 1906, p. 6.

Peguis: A Final Bargain
Letter from Peguis appears in Hind, Henry Youle. *Narrative of the Canadian Red River Exploring Expedition of 1857*. London: Longman, Green, Longman and Roberts, 1860. pp. 173–174.

Three-Dollar Bill
Adapted from the text of Treaty 1 (August 3, 1871), https://www .aadnc-aandc.gc.ca/eng/1100100028664/1100100028665 (Indigenous and Northern Affairs Canada).

Cousins
Epigraph: "Every married woman and mother of a family…." is from Alexander Kennedy Isbister's article "The Hudson's Bay Territories" in the *Nor'Wester*, August 15, 1861, p.1.

You Look Like an Indian
Alexander Peter Reid's hierarchy is referenced on Norma Jean Hall's site about the Red River Settlement: https://hallnjean2.wordpress.com. Reid's original article was published in 1874 in *Journal of the Anthropological Institute of Great Britain and Ireland*.

For a full description of patterns of genetic variation and the difficulties in assigning race, see Weiss, Kenneth M., and Jeffrey C. Long. "Non-Darwinian estimation: My ancestors, my genes' ancestors." *Genome Research*, 19 (2009): 703–710.

Selected material in this chapter and elsewhere in the book appeared earlier in Neilsen Glenn, L. "Marking the Page." *In this Together: Fifteen Stories of Truth & Reconciliation.* Danielle Metcalfe-Chenail (ed.). Victoria: Brindle and Glass, 2016. pp. 148–57.

A Nail in Old Wood

A list of the first communicants in St. Peter, Dynevor Old Stone Church appears in Sutherland, Donna G. *Peguis: A Noble Friend.* St. Andrews, MB: Chief Peguis Heritage Park, 2003. p. 134. The original source is the letters of William Cockran (PAM, CMS, A85, n.d)

Lines excerpted from Louise Bernice Halfe's "miyo-ohpikinâwa-sowin" in *Burning in this Midnight Dream.* Regina: Coteau Books, 2016. p.41.

Mere Etymology

"Halfbreed" article published in *Nor'wester,* October 22, 1862, p. 2.

Stranger Things

For more on post-mortem photography see Reilly, Jill, "Haunting Photographs of the Dead Taken in Victorian Age Shows Fad for Relatives Posing Alongside Bodies of Their Dearly Departed," *Daily Mail,* October 9, 2013: http://www.dailymail.co.uk/news/article-2450832 /Victorian-photographs-relatives-posing-alongside-dead-bodies.html

Part Two: Her Many Names

Introductory epigraph for the section from Rosanna Deerchild, "We Are Just" in *The Puritan* (http://puritan-magazine.com/we-are-just/).

Ordinary Odyssey

Matthew Cocking's journal excerpt is from *An Adventurer from Hudson Bay: Journal of Matthew Cocking, from York Factory to the*

Blackfeet Country, 1772–73. Lawrence Burpee (ed.). Sections from August and September 1772.

I have drawn on the work of Ray Beaumont for information about the connections among Matthew Cocking, William Cook, Ke-che-cho-wick and Wash-e-soo-E'Squew. Some sources claim Wash-e-soo-E'Squew is, in fact, William Cook's daughter, but Beaumont's research reveals otherwise. His original unpublished article ("Mary Cocking (Budd)") can be now found online at http://www.metismuseum.ca/media/db/10288.

Details about Wash-e-soo-E'Squew's interest in education for her children are from Tolly Bradford's *Prophetic Identities: Indigenous Missionaries on British Colonial Frontiers, 1850–75.* Vancouver: UBC Press, 2012, pp 18-20.

A Lineage of Foremothers: 1758 to 1908
Joanne Arnott's "Truth and Wreck" can be found online at https://www.wpm2011.org/node/553.

Wanted: Fur Trade Wife
Epigraph from Garry Thomas Morse's "Squaw" in *Prairie Harbour.* Vancouver: Talonbooks, 2015. p. 64.

Woman with an Axe
Excerpted from *David Thompson's Narrative of his Explorations of Western America, 1784–1812.* Toronto: Champlain Society XII, c. 1916.

Wash-e-soo-E'Squew Cocking (later, Mary Budd)
Letter from W.H. Cook in Beaumont, Ray. "Mary Cocking (Budd)." Online at http://www.metismuseum.ca/media/db/10288.

Bride

This testamentum is from Lamb, W. Kaye (ed.). *Sixteen Years in the Indian Country: The Journal of David Williams Harmon, 1800–1816.* Toronto: Macmillan, 1957.

Dressed

Testamentum excerpted from Lamb, W. Kaye (ed.). *The Journals and Letters of Sir Alexander Mackenzie.* London: Cambridge University Press, 1970.

One of the Ingrates

Adapted from the journal of the Reverend Abraham Cowley. Church Missionary Society Records. F.W. Rice Fonds. Library and Archives Canada (mfm at PAC, MG 19, E9).

A Bird in the Bush

Passage adapted from Ross, Alexander. *The Red River Settlement: Its Rise, Progress, and Present State.* London: Smith, Elder and Company, 1856.

Catherine (Kitty) Budd Erasmus

Adapted from Erasmus, Peter (with Henry Thompson). *Buffalo Days and Nights.* Calgary: Fifth House, 1999.

Niwikimakan: Life with a Man

From *The Substance of a Journal during a Residence at the Red River Colony British North America; and frequent excursions among the North-West American Indians, in the years 1820, 1821, 1822, 1823* by Reverend John West, M.A., late chaplain to the Hudson's Bay Company. London: L. B. Seeley and Son, 1824.

Following the River

Instructions for Turning Off

Material adapted from the following sources:

Donald McKenzie quote from Van Kirk, Sylvia. *Many Tender Ties*. Winnipeg: Watson and Dwyer Publishing, 1980. p. 180.

"Commodity" quote from Welsh, Christine. "Women in the Shadows: Reclaiming a Métis Heritage." *New Contexts of Canadian Criticism.* Ajay Heble, Donna Palmateer Pennee and J.R. Struthers (eds). Peterborough, ON: Broadview Press, 1999. p. 63.

"Sow" comment made by a company officer found in Galbraith, John S. *The Little Emperor: Governor Simpson of the Hudson's Bay Company.* Toronto: Macmillan, 1976.

People on the Stage

From Hargrave, Letitia. *The letters of Letitia Hargrave.* Margaret Arnett MacLeod (ed.). Toronto: The Champlain Society, 1947. pp. 58–64.

Teacher

Adapted from a number of sources including Glazebrook, G.P. de T. (ed.). *The Hargrave Correspondence: 1821–1843.* Toronto: The Champlain Society, 1938; Van Kirk, Sylvia. *Many Tender Ties.* Winnipeg: Watson and Dwyer Publishing, 1980; and Calloway, Colin G. *White People, Indians, and Highlanders.* New York: Oxford University Press, 2008.

Tall Poppy: How to Write a Red River Tragedy

Many versions and interpretations of Sarah Ballenden's story exist – I have drawn from several, including George Ingram's short biography of Eden Colvile, available online at http://parkscanadahistory.com/series/chs/4/chs4-3g.htm, as well as accounts by Sylvia Van Kirk, Frits Pannekoek, Maureen Hunter and others.

Devoted Labourer
Commentary about Sophia's death drawn from *The Church Missionary Gleaner New Series*, vol 11. London: Seeley, Jackson, and Halliday, 1861.

Dusky Worshippers
Adapted from Hind, Henry Youle. *Narrative of the Canadian Red River Exploring Expedition of 1857*. London: Longman, Green, Longman and Roberts, 1860.

Oayache Mannin
Steps for the jig can be found under "Red River jig" at the Virtual Museum of Canada (www.virtualmuseum.ca). Some details for this piece are from *Harper's* magazine, October 1860.

Travels with Harriet
Adapted from Healy, W.J. *Women of Red River*. Winnipeg: Russell, Lang & Co. Ltd., 1923. (Public domain.)
   Research by historian Norma J. Hall indicates the Cowans left Red River during the time of the resistance, Dr. Cowan to attend to HBC business and Mrs. Cowan to return to England to pick up their children, who were being educated there.

Backbiters
Charles Mair is quoted in Hargrave, Joseph. *Red River*. Montreal: John Lovell, 1871. p. 454.

Woman with a Backbone
Material adapted from Lamirande, Todd. "Annie McDermot, (Bannatyne)." Compiled and edited by Lawrence Barkwell, Louis Riel Institute. Online at http://www.metismuseum.ca/media/db/07426

Mama is an Indian
Based on a letter from James Ross to his sister, Jemima. Sally Timentwa Ross was the daughter of an Okanagan chief and had at least twelve children with Alexander Ross. Jemima may have felt adolescent embarrassment about a parent; historian Sylvia Van Kirk's account leans toward a racist interpretation of the church incident.

Elizabeth Setter Norquay
Adapted from Healy, W.J. *Women of Red River.* Winnipeg: Russell, Lang, 1923. (Public domain.)

Maria Thomas: Infernal Liar
Details of this story, including testimonies of participants, have been compiled from several sources, including editions of the *Nor'Wester* newspaper March–May 1863; Hargrave, Joseph James. *Red River.* Montreal: John Lovell, 1871; McCormick, Chris, and Len Green (eds). *Crime and Deviance in Canada.* Toronto: Canadian Scholars' Press, 2005; Gibson, Dale. *Law, Life, and Government at Red River, Volume 2: General Quarterly Court of Assiniboia, Annotated Records, 1844–1872.* Montreal: McGill-Queen's University Press, 2015; and others.

Griffith Owen Corbett's wife, Abigail, is listed in the 1870 census with her four children. The youngest child, Mary Eliza, was born in 1862. Some historians speculate Mary Eliza was, in fact, Maria Thomas's child by Corbett. Others speculate Maria's parents, the Thomases, raised Maria's child.

Patient Wife
1879 article about Antoine Couture in *Manitoba Free Press*, August 9, Volume VII, Number 30 (front page).

Upright: Or, Intelligence Comes to Red River
Adapted from MacBeth, R.G. *The Romance of Western Canada*. Toronto: William Briggs, 1918. p. 84.

The Girl Who Loved You So True
Historian Edith Fowke claims the song was composed at the time of the Wolseley Expedition and told the story of a Métis girl lamenting the departure of her Anglo lover. The text of the song was discovered in the papers of a former Royal Canadian Mounted Police officer, Colonel Gilbert Sanders. Letters by Wolseley and Riel are taken verbatim from the *Manitoba Free Press*, including, in the case of Wolseley's letter, spelling errors. On July 15, 1870, Rupert's Land and the Northwest Territories were transferred into Canadian hands.

Enfranchise
I have drawn from the following sources:
Chelsea Vowel quote from *Indigenous Writes: A Guide to First Nations, Métis & Inuit Issues in Canada*. Winnipeg: Portage and Main Press, 2016. p. 28.
  Junior Liberal Association meeting debate on women's suffrage, *Brandon Sun Weekly*, March 25, 1886.

Enfranchise, 1959–1985
Parts of this text were published as "All Your Hands Were Verbs" by Lorri Neilsen Glenn in *Prairie Fire*, Spring 2016.

Town Kisser
This comment appears in the article "Around Selkirk in 1882" by George D. Gibbs in *Selkirk's 75th Anniversary* (1957), a community publication.

Following the River

Where They Cannot Find Her: May 12, 1885
Adapted from Barkwell, Lawrence J. *Women of the 1885 Resistance*.
Winnipeg: Louis Riel Institute, 2012. p. 20.

Doing Laundry in the Resistance
Adapted from Barkwell, Lawrence J. *Women of the 1885 Resistance*.
Winnipeg: Louis Riel Institute, 2012. p. 56.

Sister Annie Goulet
Sources include McGuire, Rita. "The Grey Sisters in the Red River Settlement." *CCHA, Historical Studies* 53 (1986): 21–37; and Mitchell, Es-
telle. *Les Grey Nuns and the Red River Settlement*. Service des archives
et des collections Soeurs de la Charité de Montréal, 2014. (Digital edition in public domain.)

Taché quote from Lesley Erickson's "Repositioning the Missionary:
Sara Riel, the Grey Nuns, and Aboriginal Women in Catholic Missions
of the Northwest." In Carter, Sarah, and Patricia Alice McCormack
(eds). *Recollecting: Lives of Aboriginal women of the Canadian North-
west*, Edmonton: Athabasca University Press, 2011. p. 126.

The Indian Question: What Settler Women Say
From an 1886 survey: *What Women say of the Canadian North-West:
A Simple Statement of the Experiences of Women Settled in all Parts
of Manitoba and the North-West Territories*. The survey was part of
Canada's efforts to increase immigration to the West.

Don't Spoil Your Looks
Article from *Brandon Daily Sun*, December 22, 1904.

All the Names
Testamentum from Reverend R. G. MacBeth in his book *The Selkirk
Settlers in Real Life*. Toronto: William Briggs, 1897. pp. 58–59.

Once Upon a Bird

Sandhill Crane quote from Charette, Guillaume. *Vanishing Spaces: Memoirs of a Prairie Métis.* Translated by Ray Ellenwood. Winnipeg: Editions Bois-Brûles, 1976. p. 37.

Blackbird quote (Mary Wells) from Ahenakew, Freda, and H.C. Wolfart. *Kôhkominawak Otâcimowiniwâwa: Our Grandmothers' Lives as Told in Their Own Words.* University of Regina: Canada Plains Research Centre, 1998. p. 171.

Bird Jelly for Convalescents from *Selkirk's 75th Anniversary.* Town of Selkirk Community Publication, 1957. p. 8.

Goose Soup recipe from *Indigenous Food First*: Online at http://iffculture.ca/recipe/goose-soup/. Hydro project impact statement from the Grand Council of the Crees website (http://www.gcc.ca).

Klondike Kitty

Newspaper articles from *Dawson Record*, September 15, 1903 and April 3, 1908.

Part Three: The Road Back
School

Parts of this section have appeared earlier in Neilsen Glenn, L. "Marking the Page." *In this Together: Fifteen Stories of Truth & Reconciliation.* Danielle Metcalfe-Chenail (ed.). Victoria: Brindle and Glass, 2016. pp. 148–157.

Epigraphs from Elder Betsy Anderson, Tadoule Lake, Manitoba, and Chelsea Vowel (âpihtawikosisân) from blogpost of August 22, 2013, online at http://apihtawikosisan.com/2013/08/we-cant-get-anywhere-until-we-flip-the-narrative/.

Excerpt from Dumont, Marilyn. "The Devil's Language." *A Really Good Brown Girl.* London, ON: Brick Books, 1996. p. 54.

Quotes are from Richard Wagamese (Speakingmytruth.ca), from Duncan Campbell Scott's poem "The Half-Breed Girl" and from the amendment to the Indian Act requiring all Indigenous children to attend residential school. The Canadian Museum of History exhibition *100 Years of Loss: Healing the Legacy of the Residential Schools* is a travelling display about Canadian residential schools that launched in 2014.

The Road Back
Epigraph from Halfe, Louise Bernice (Sky Dancer). "oskwāpam – the pipe." *Burning in this Midnight Dream.* Regina: Coteau Books, 2016. p. 66.

Moniyaw is a Cree word for white person (variations include môniyaw, moniyâw, môniyâw).

Wêmistikôsowak means white man who crossed the sea with wooden boats. Another possible term is *Kakêpâcisk*, which translates as dumb bum.

My aim here is to capture white people's behaviour that causes eye-rolling or head-shaking.

Source for Cree: Ann-Margaret Day-Osborne.

Crooked Tongue
Quote from Chief Cathy Merrick appears in a CBC article online October 17, 2014, at http://www.cbc.ca/news/canada/manitoba/manitoba-hydro-evicted-from-northern-dam-station-1.2803462.

Inquiry, 1908 (all selections)
All testimony documented here appears verbatim (with minor alterations for consistency and readability) from coverage of the inquiry by the *Winnipeg Tribune,* September 1908.

Ship's Cat
This piece is a response to an article in *Lögberg-Heimskringla,* Friday, March 3, 2000, by Clifford Stevens. Much of the information in the

article is inconsistent with documented testimony at the SS *Premier* inquiry in the fall of 1908. The October 19, 1908, edition of the *Montreal Gazette* reported on the captain's actions.

The Way a Landscape Writes Itself

David Abram quotes are from his book *Becoming Animal: An Earthly Cosmology.* New York: Random House, 2011. p. 171.

One name for Northern peoples is kinosêwisipîwininiwak. An alternate name is kenosao sipik ininiwak.

Part Four: Night Fishing
Night Fishing

Written in response to an article from CBC news, July 1, 2015. "Couple Reels in Clump of Hair from River in Winnipeg." Online at http://www.cbc.ca/news/canada/manitoba/couple-reels-in-clump-of-hair-from-river-in-winnipeg-1.3134573L

Blanket Statements

Selections are from Ross, Alexander. *The Red River Settlement: Its Rise, Progress, and Present State.* London: Smith, Elder, & Co., 1856. p. 191; Campbell, Maria. *Halfbreed.* Toronto: McClelland and Stewart, 1973. p. 159; and Emily Kematch in *Final Report: Truth and Reconciliation Commission of Canada* (The Survivors Speak), 2015. p. 81.

Of Middens and Graves

Epigraphs from Harrison, Robert Pogue. *The Dominion of the Dead.* Chicago: University of Chicago Press, 2003. p. ix; and Wells, Mary, quoted in *Kôhkominawak Otâcimowiniwâwa: Our Grandmothers' Lives as Told in Their Own Words.* University of Regina: Canada Plains Research Centre, 1998. p. 183.

James Isham's quote on burial practices from his *Observations on Hudson's Bay, 1743, and Notes and Observations on a Book Entitled*

Following the River

A Voyage to Hudson's Bay, 1749. Edited by E.E. Rich. Millwood, NY: Kraus International Publications, 1969. Rough population numbers from the Population Reference Bureau in Washington, DC.

Quote from Blair, Peggy. *The Non-Protection of Canadian Aboriginal Heritage Burial and Artifacts.* The Scow Institute, 2005. p. 3. Available online at http://scow-archive.libraries.coop/library/documents/HeritageSitesFacts.pdf.

Canadian Museum of Human Rights story from *Winnipeg Sun,* August 28, 2013.

Learning
Calls for action interspersed in this section are from the Truth and Reconciliation report.

By Water
Epigraphs from Le Guin, Ursula K. "The Art of Fiction No. 221" interview with John Wray in *The Paris Review,* 206 (Fall 2013); and Vermette, Katherena. "Family." *North End Love Songs.* Winnipeg: The Muses Company, 2012. p. 52.

Afterword
Comments by Gregory Scofield used with permission. Comment by Tracey Lindberg about caring for one other was part of her address to the Canadian Creative Writers and Writing Programs conference, June 10, 2017, in Fredericton, NB.

Glossary

Cree: The accounts in this book are set in different geographical locations; as a result, words from different dialects of Cree appear in this manuscript. Cree words have been checked by a Cree language instructor in Norway House and by local speakers. Any incorrect uses, variations or deviations from accepted use are entirely my responsibility.

âtayôhkanak – spiritual helpers, including grandparents
kinosêwisîpîwininiwak – a term for the Norway House Cree
kinosêwisîpiy (also *kinosao sipi*) – Norway House
maskêkowininiwak – a term for Northern Swampy Cree
nêhiyawêwin – Plains Cree dialect
nêyawahahk – Warren's Landing
nipiy ôma pimâtisiwin – water is life
niwikimikan – marriage partner
Oayache Mannin – Michif term for Red River jig
wêmistikôsowak – white man who crossed the sea on wooden boats

Other terms:
tha uisge na beatha – Water of life (Not to be confused with the Gaelic terms for whisky: uisge beatha [Scottish dialect] and uisce beatha [Irish dialect]).

Bibliography

Acoose, Janice. *Iskwewak-Kah'Ki Yaw Ni Wahkomakanak: Neither Indian Princesses Nor Easy Squaws*. Toronto: Women's Press, 1975.

Ahenakew, Freda & H.C. Wolfart. *Kôhkominawak Otâcimowiniwâwa: Our Grand-mothers' Lives as Told in Their Own Words*. University of Regina: Canada Plains Research Centre, 1998.

Aiken, Don. *It Happened in Manitoba*. Calgary: Fifth House, 2004.

Arnott, Joanne. "Truth and Wreck." Poem commissioned by the Centre for Dialogue at Simon Fraser University (written in honour of Chief Robert Joseph). Found at https://www.sfu.ca/dialogue/watch-read-discover/reconciliation-chief-robert-joseph/reconciliation-poetry/arnott-poem.html, 2014.

Barkwell, Lawrence J., and Darren R. Préfontaine. *A Métis Studies Bibliography: Annotated Bibliography and References*. Winnipeg: Gabriel Dumont Institute Press, 2016.

Barkwell, Lawrence J. *Women of the 1885 Resistance*. Winnipeg: Louis Riel Institute, 2012.

Barris, Theodore. *Fire Canoe: Prairie Steamboat Days Revisited*. Toronto: McClelland and Stewart, 1977.

Beaumont, Ray, and Lawrence J. Barkwell. *Mary Cocking (Budd)*. Winnipeg: Louis Riel Institute, 2009.

Begg, Alexander. *Alexander Begg's Red River Journal, and Other Papers Relative to the Red River Resistance 1869–70*, edited by W. L. Morton. Toronto: Champlain Society, 1956.

Bradford, Tolly. *Prophetic Identities: Indigenous Missionaries on British Colonial Frontiers*. Vancouver: University of British Columbia Press, 2012.

Bumsted, J. M. *Thomas Scott's Body and Other Essays on Early Manitoba History*. Winnipeg: University of Manitoba Press, 2000.

Calloway, Colin. *White People, Indians, and Highlanders*. Oxford and New York: Oxford University Press, 2008.

Campbell, Maria. *Halfbreed*. Toronto: McClelland and Stewart, 1973.

Following the River

Campbell, Marjorie Wilkins. *The Nor'westers*. Toronto: Macmillan of Canada, 1974.

Campy, Lucille. *The Silver Chief*. Toronto: Natural Heritage Books, 2003.

Carpenter, Jock. *Fifty Dollar Bride: Marie Rose Smith – A Chronicle of Métis Life in the 19th Century*. Sidney, BC: Gray's Publishing Ltd., 1971.

Carter, Sarah, and Patricia Alice McCormack. *Recollecting: Lives of Aboriginal women of the Canadian Northwest and Borderlands*. Edmonton: Athabasca University Press, 2011.

Charette, Guillaume. *Vanishing Spaces: Memoirs of a Prairie Métis*. Translated by Ray Ellenwood. Winnipeg: Editions Bois-Brûlés, 1976.

Cherney, Bruce. "Tragic Sinking of SS *Princess* – Called First Major Maritime Disaster on Lake Winnipeg." Winnipeg: *Real Estate News*, June 1, 2007

Coates, Ta-Nehisi. *Between the World and Me*. New York: Random House, 2015.

Cocking, Matthew. *An Adventurer from Hudson Bay: Journal of Matthew Cocking, from York Factory to the Blackfeet Country, 1772–1773*. Edited and with an introduction by Lawrence Burpee. Ottawa: Royal Society of Canada, 1909.

Coutts, Robert. *The Road to the Rapids: Nineteenth Century Church and Society at St. Andrew's Parish, Red River*. Calgary: University of Calgary Press, 2000.

Daniels, Harry W. *The Forgotten People*. Ottawa: The Native Council of Canada, 1979.

Daschuk, James. *Clearing the Plains*. Regina: University of Regina Press, 2013.

Deerchild, Rosanna. *calling down the sky*. Markham, ON: Bookland Press, 2015.

Dumont, Marilyn. *The Pemmican Eaters*. Toronto: ECW Press, 2015.

———. *Green Girl Dreams Mountains*. Lantzville, BC: Oolichan Books, 2001.

———. *A Really Good Brown Girl*. London, ON: Brick Books, 1996.

Erasmus, Peter, Jr., with Henry Thompson. *Buffalo Days and Nights*. Calgary: Fifth House, 1999.

Francis, R. Douglas, and Howard Palmer (Eds). *The Prairie West: Historical Readings*. Edmonton: The University of Alberta Press, 1992.

Gibson, Dale. *Law, Life and Government at Red River*. Vol. 2, *General Quarterly Court of Assiniboia Annotated Records*. 1844–1872. Montreal: McGill-Queen's University Press, 2015.

Glazebrook, G. P. de T., ed. *The Hargrave Correspondence*. Toronto: The Champlain Society, 1938.

Green, Wilson F. *Red River Revelations* Winnipeg: Hignell Printing (Red River Valley International Centennial), 1974.

Halfe, Louise Bernice. *Burning in this Midnight Dream*. Regina: Coteau Books, 2016.

Hall, Norma J. https://hallnjean2.wordpress.com

———. https://casualtyofcolonialism.wordpress.com.

———. "A Perfect Freedom: Red River as a Settler Society 1810-1870." Thesis in partial fulfillment of the Requirements for the Degree of Master of Arts, Department of History, University of Manitoba, 2003.

Hargrave, Joseph. *Red River.* Montreal: John Lovell, 1871.

Hargrave, Letitia. *The letters of Letitia Hargrave.* Toronto: The Champlain Society, 1947.

Harrison, Robert Pogue. *The Dominion of the Dead.* Chicago: University of Chicago Press, 2003.

Healy, W. J. *Women of Red River.* Winnipeg: Russell, Lang & Co. Ltd., 1923.

Hind, Henry Youle. *Narrative of the Canadian Red River Exploring Expedition of 1857.* London: Longman, Green, Longman and Roberts, 1860.

Hogan, Linda. *Dwellings: A Spiritual History of the Living World.* New York: Touchstone Books, 1996.

Isham, James. *Observations on Hudson's Bay, 1743, and Notes and Observations on a Book Entitled A Voyage to Hudson's Bay, 1749.* Edited by E. E. Rich. Millwood, NY: Kraus International Publications, 1969.

Keating, William H. *Narrative of an Expedition to the Source of the St. Peter's River, Lake Winnepeek, Lake of the Woods &c. &c.,* vol. 2. Philadelphia: H.C. Carey and I. Lea, 1824.

Kreutzweiser, E. E. *The Red River Insurrection.* Gardenvale, QC.: The Garden City Press, 1936.

Lamb, W. Kaye, ed. *The Journals and Letters of Alexander MacKenzie.* London: Cambridge University Press, 1970.

———. *Sixteen Years in the Indian Country: The Journal of Daniel Williams Harmon, 1800–1816.* Macmillan: Toronto, 1957.

Lamirande, Todd. "Annie McDermot (Bannatyne)." Compiled and edited by Lawrence Barkwell. Winnipeg: The Louis Riel Institute, 2008.

MacBeth, R.G. *The Romance of Western Canada.* Toronto: William Briggs, 1918.

MacBeth, R.G. *The Selkirk Settlers in Real Life.* Toronto: William Briggs, 1897.

MacDonald, Malcolm. *Canadian North.* London: Oxford University Press, 1945.

MacLeod, R. C. *Swords and Ploughshares.* Edmonton: The University of Alberta Press, 1993.

Mackenzie, Alexander. *The Journals and Letters of Sir Alexander MacKenzie.* Edited by W. Kaye Lamb. London: Cambridge University Press (for the Hakluyt Society), 1970.

McCormick, Chris and Green, Len, eds. *Crime and Deviance in Canada.* Toronto: Canadian Scholars' Press, 2005.

McGilchrist, Iain. *The Master and His Emissary.* New Haven, CT: Yale University Press, 2009.

Morin, Gail. *Métis Families: A Genealogical Compendium.* Pawtucket, RI: Quintin Publications, 2001.

———. *Censuses of the Red River Settlement (1827–1843).* Pawtucket, RI: Quintin Publications, 1998.

Municipality of St. Andrew's. *Beyond the Gates of Lower Fort Garry.* Clandeboye, MB: Friesen Printing for Municipality of St. Andrew's, 1982.

Neilsen Glenn, Lorri. "Marking the Page." *In This Together: Fifteen Stories of Truth & Reconciliation.* Edited by Danielle Metcalfe-Chenail. Victoria: Brindle and Glass, 2015.

Pannekoek, Frits. *A Snug Little Flock: The Social Origins of the Riel Resistance of 1869-70.* Chicago: Watson and Dwyer, 1991.

Peterson, Jacqueline, and Jennifer Brown. *The New Peoples.* Winnipeg: The University of Manitoba Press International Centennial (1974–1976), 1985.

Pettipas, Katherine. *The Diary of Henry Budd.* Manitoba Record Society Publications. General Editor W. D. Smith. Winnipeg: Hignell Printing, 1974.

Potyondi, Barry. *Selkirk: The First Hundred Years.* Winnipeg: Josten's Services, 1981.

Pritchett, John Perry. *The Red River Valley: 1811–1849.* Toronto: Ryerson Press, 1942.

Robertson, David Alexander. *Scars,* Book 1. Winnipeg: Highwater Press, 2010.

———. *Stone,* Book 2. Winnipeg: Highwater Press, 2010.

———. *Ends/Begins,* Book 3. Winnipeg: Highwater Press, 2010.

———. *The Pact,* Book 4. Winnipeg: Highwater Press, 2011.

Ross, Eric. *Beyond the River and the Bay.* Toronto: University of Toronto Press, 1970.

Ross, Alexander. *The Red River Settlement: Its Rise, Progress, and Present State.* London: Smith, Elder & Co., 1856.

Scofield, Gregory. *I Knew Two Métis Women.* Vancouver: Polestar Books, 1999.

Sellars, Bev. *They Called Me Number One.* Vancouver: Talon Books, 2013.

Sutherland, Donna G. *Peguis: A Noble Friend.* Manitoba: Derksen Publishing, 1993.

Thomas Morse, Garry. *Prairie Harbour.* Vancouver: Talonbooks, 2015.

Thompson, David. *David Thompson's Narrative of his Explorations in Western America 1784–1812.* Toronto: Champlain Society XII, 1916.

Trémaudan, Auguste Henri de. *Hold High your Heads.* Winnipeg, MB: Pemmican Publications, 1982.

Van Kirk, Sylvia. "The impact of white women in fur trade society." In *Sweet Promises: A Reader on Indian-White Relations in Canada,* edited by J.R. Miller. Toronto: University of Toronto Press, 1991.

———. *Many Tender Ties.* Winnipeg: Watson and Dwyer Publishing, 1980.

Vermette, Katherena. *North End Love Songs.* Winnipeg: The Muses Company, 2012.

Vowel, Chelsea (âpihtawikosisân). *Indigenous Writes*. Winnipeg: Portage and Main Press, 2016.

Weiss, Kenneth M., and Jeffrey Long. "Non-Darwinian estimation: My ancestors, my genes' ancestors." *Genome Research*. 19 (2009).

Welsh, Christine. "Women in the Shadows: Reclaiming a Métis Heritage" in *New Contexts of Canadian Criticism*, ed. Ajay Heble, Donna Palmateer Pennee, J.R. Struthers, p. 60. Peterborough: Broadview Press, 1997.

West, Reverend John. *The Substance of a Journal during a Residence at the Red River Colony British North America; and Frequent Excursions among the North-West American Indians, in the years 1820, 1821, 1822, 1823*. London: L.B. Seeley and Son, Fleet Street, 1824.